NADIA G'S Bitchin' Kitchen COOKBOOK

ROCK YOUR KITCHEN
AND LET THE BOYS CLEAN UP THE MESS

by: Nadia Giosia

skirt!

GUILFORD, CONNECTICUT

An imprint of The Globe Pequot Press

This cookbook is dedicated to my Mom, Josh, and hungry bad-girls everywhere.

To buy books in quantity for corporate use
or incentives, call **(800) 962–0973**
or e-mail **premiums@GlobePequot.com.**

Copyright © 2009 by B360 Media, Inc.

ALL RIGHTS RESERVED. No part of this book may be reproduced or transmitted in any form by any
means, electronic or mechanical, including photocopying and recording, or by any information
storage and retrieval system, except as may be expressly permitted in writing from the publisher.
Requests for permission should be addressed to The Globe Pequot Press, Attn: Rights and
Permissions Department, P.O. Box 480, Guilford, CT 06437.

skirt!® is an imprint of The Globe Pequot Press.

skirt! is a registered trademark of Morris Publishing Group, LLC,
and is used with express permission.

Due to limitations of space, additional art credits appear on pp. 206–7 and constitute an extension
of this page.

Library of Congress Cataloging-in-Publication Data is available on file.

ISBN 978-1-59921-441-2

Printed in the United States of America

10 9 8 7 6 5 4 3 2 1

NADIA G'S Bitchin Kitchen COOKBOOK

CONTENTS

Righteous Introduction

My uncle Pashqua used to say, "Any occasion is a good occasion for a meal." No one was ever more right . . . or sweaty.

As an Italian, I know that a good meal isn't reserved for just Hallmark holidays, pretentious dinner parties, or . . . some other example because comedy works best in threes. Oh no! *Every day* there's a good reason to *shkoff! From One-Night-Stand Breakfasts to Dump 'Em Desserts, this cookbook focuses on the *other occasions*—the daily dish that's relevant to a new generation who simply don't give a flying fuck about stuffing a turkey in the name of pillaging.

And when these overlooked occasions arise, you've got to celebrate, devise, deal. And what better way to deal, than to stuff your face like a savage? Food brings your friends, family, and thighs closer together. It can soften a blow, get you your way, or channel your rage. Food gives us a reason to wake up in the morning (and eat breakfast), visit our grandparents, stay in crappy relationships! And that's what this cookbook explores at its very core: the connection between food, circumstance, and greased-up chiseled man babes. . . . What was my point again?

Oh yeah . . . Bitchin' Kitchen! But it goes even deeper than that! It's about me, I mean "us." It's about Net Genners, Punk-Italian Fusion, and Angry Squirrels. It's about kicking polite pastel lifestyles in the ass, rocking your kitchen, and letting the boys clean up the mess.

I know what you're thinking: "Is that my cell phone ringing?" Of course it is! But I don't care, because *this* is a righteous introduction. So sit back, take off at least one of your socks, and get ready to get your hands dirty, because you're going to shkoff like you've never shkoffed before! (Or you can always just look at the pretty pictures. Come on, everybody likes pictures.)

XoX

*NOTE:

Whenever you see an asterisk, it means you can check the Glossary for a definition of this saying—that's if you're not already familiar with Italian-American slang, *capisce?

The Hand that Rocks the Ladle

When I was growing up I was always jealous of my mom's prowess in the kitchen: the way she'd be able to whack me with a slipper as she answered the phone, all the while pouring a steady stream of salt into the pasta water, just *feeling* the perfect amount. It was witchcraft! She never had a measuring cup; I never saw her meticulously quantify ⅛ of a teaspoon of anything. Ever. Around the house there were no written recipes, nor at my *Nonna's, or at her Nonna's[1]. If you were to ask my mother how much salt goes into a quart of water, she'd tell you, annoyed: "*Ma, what do I know?! You look, you feel, you taste." And that was that. You look, you feel, you taste.

I was so aggravated by this as a teen that I rebelled against the *Casalinga style of Italian cooking, snatching up any recipe that had irrefutable amounts, bullet points, friggin' diagrams! And with this arsenal of *tangible* instructions in hand, I set out to vengefully make the biggest, best meal anyone had ever tasted.... Oh, and if someone were to ask *me* how much salt *I* used, I'd cordially reply: "Why, 1.78 teaspoons, Madame . . . " But no one ever asked, because all those meals sucked. They sucked hard, and sucked for years. They never came together. Maybe I was following the wrong recipes, or maybe it takes more than a set of measuring spoons to make a good meal. Maybe it is witchcraft.

Is the Hand that Rules the World

. . . Or knowing your ingredients. And how do you get to know your ingredients? Well, *you look, you feel, you taste*. By trial and error, you realize that a whole head of garlic for 1 cup of tomato puree is a bit much. You make a mental note. And as you sit there, defiantly shkoffing a plate of nasty pasta, hoping that the next forkful will miraculously reveal itself as delicious, getting progressively more full, and progressively more aware of how much fucking garlic is in this godforsaken sauce, you learn. It haunts you, from the mess in the kitchen to the hole in your wallet to the indigestion. Some of us give up at this point, figure we'll never learn to cook and order out for the rest of our days.

But some of us don't. Some of us rise up to the challenge because food is too important. It was the first thing that ever gave you comfort, before sex, drugs, or rock and roll. Because the pleasure you get from eating or watching someone succumb to your culinary genius is too primal, too satisfying, too powerful to ever not hold in the crook of your wooden spoon.

It's witchcraft baby.

nadmit

[1] We did own "The Good Housekeeping Illustrated Cookbook," which was used once for a fashionably bland curry in the mid-80s. It then got buried in the Wedding/Communion/Confirmation video drawer and was never seen again.

The Bitchin' Basics

ORGANIC INGREDIENTS

Always try to get your hands on organic-certified ingredients. Don't get me wrong, this isn't a hippie cookbook, but I'm a firm believer that you shouldn't put anything in your mouth that's chock-full of sketchy hormones, antibiotics, or chemicals (past the age of 19.) Almost all cities have a farmer's market and this is where the best ingredients are found. But beware, just because you're at the farmer's market doesn't mean everything is organic, so if you're not sure, ask.

I know it's not easy to eat 100% organic, so if I had to put my foot down on certain ingredients it would be the meat. Never cook with *cac meat. But you probably won't listen to me, so . . .

BURGER STINK JUICE

Sometimes the ground beef you find at the grocery store isn't top-notch, and when you sauté it you notice a watery liquid at the bottom of the pan. This liquid smells like a cross between expired margarine and death. Strain this liquid, keep cooking the beef, then strain some more until it's all gone. Or better yet, listen to me and only buy fresh organic beef from a certified butcher.

OLIVE OIL

There are three things you never want to be stingy about: sky-diving, plastic surgery, and olive oil. Since olive oil is found in almost every Mediterranean dish, don't be penny-wise and pound foolish. Buy the best quality, cold-pressed, extra virgin olive oil you can afford, otherwise you'll ruin a great meal. (I usually shell out between $15 and $25 for a 500 ml bottle of extra virgin.)

BUTTER

Don't buy salted butter. You're the master of your kitchen, so you control the salt. Also know that margarine *isn't* a replacement for butter, it's Satan's lube. Not only is this crap nasty-tasting, it's extremely unhealthy. Margarine is made from some of the the cheapest oils on earth, barely fit for human consumption. These scavenger oils are then processed with chemicals, bleached, deodorized, and finally dyed an "appetizing" yellow color. I can't believe it's not shoe polish.

DEGERMING GARLIC

Most garlic is shipped all the way from China and by the time it reaches the grocery store shelves it has already begun to germinate. This germ, located in the center of the clove, infests your recipes with a dark, overly-ripe garlic flavor that you'll keep burping up for hours. Ideally you want to buy young organic garlic that has no germ. But whenever that's not a possibility, abort the sucker.

PASTA & SAUCE

Pasta is best when you follow these steps: (1) Cook it al dente (about 8 to 10 minutes, depending on the kind of pasta). (2) Boil it in sufficiently salted water, about as salty as you like your soup. (3) Once the pasta is cooked, strain it, pour it into a big bowl and mix it with a ladleful of sauce so every strand absorbs some saucy goodness. (4) Go easy on the sauce. You're supposed to be tasting the pasta and highlighted ingredients, not tomato soup. Two to three tablespoons of sauce is enough for 1 cup of cooked pasta.

ADDING SPICES

Cooking is a tactile experience for me and I quantify by using big or small *pinches. By running the spices between my fingertips I feel the perfect amount (gawd, we all turn into our mothers don't we?) This takes practice, so if you're new to the kitchen remember that less is more. You can always add salt and spice if it's too bland, but you can't take any away, so be careful. (If you really need specific instructions, know that a small pinch is about ¼ of a teaspoon. A big pinch is about ½ a teaspoon.)

SEA SALT & FRESHLY CRACKED PEPPER

I always use sea salt in my recipes, it's more subtle and natural than table salt. Table salt has weird-ass additives like sodium silicoaluminate and alumnio-calcium silicate. The general rule is: if you can't pronounce it and it's in your own language, don't eat it. When it comes to peppering your dishes, there's no substitute for freshly cracked pepper. Pre-cracked pepper sits around in the open for too long and by the time it hits your plate it's lost 99 percent of its flavor. Useless.

SUGAR

Stay away from refined (bleached) sugar. Personally, I don't even know why they still carry this crap on the shelves. Bleached products come from a time where a bunch of nerdy white dudes got overly-excited by the industrial revolution and messed around with perfectly good ingredients just so they could feel omnipotent at any cost, even our health. (Don't even get me started on tampons . . .) White isn't "pure," it's dangerous.

OK! So it's best to use brown sugar, raw cane sugar, honey, or molasses to sweeten your dishes. These darker, more natural sugars don't only add sweetness, they add flavor—and flavor is always good.

CINNAMON

Never buy cinnamon in powdered form. That stuff is the anthrax of the spice world, just one airborne pinch and it's all over! Everything will be infected with the smell of cinnamon: other spices, cereals, pastas . . . even your soul. Buy cinnamon in sticks, grate them only when needed, and then store them in an airtight, bulletproof safe, two feet underground in the backyard.

NEWBIES

If you're a real newbie, then turn to page 190 for everything you need to get started. From how to stock a fridge, to essential cooking gear, to spice rack must-haves, I've got you covered.

The Kitchen Code

FEARLESSNESS

Every time I get a new knife or grater or use any sharp metal kitchen contraption for the first time, I get cut. So will you. Be prepared to get spritzed with hot oil, scalded with boiling water, suffer second-degree burns from cast-iron pans . . . but don't fret, pretty soon you won't feel it anymore and your tough hands will become a badge of honor . . . or a gnarled mess, whatever.

PATIENCE

Take the time to julienne the peppers, cube the potatoes, mince the garlic, make a basil chiffonade. Straight guys are especially bad at this, "A potato is a potato, just rub it on your t-shirt, peel off a few strands of skin and slap it in the pan, right?" Wrong. All these little prep steps are super important: Not only do they affect cook-time, but ingredients are passive-aggressive. If you don't pay attention to them, they'll get you back when dinner is served. *Hisss.*

CREATIVITY

In the culinary world nothing is written in stone. If a recipe calls for a big pinch of sugar, you may like two or none at all. So always taste as you go, involve yourself with the different layers of flavor, make adjustments, make it yours. Unless you have really bad taste, then just follow the directions.

LOVE

Cheesy as it may sound, it's true. The more you watch a sauce, fuss, and carefully stir, the better it tastes. (Psst–If anyone asks, I didn't tell you this.)

let's get cooking.

The Single Life

eing single is great! Doing what you want, when you want; flirting with hot strangers; feeling that tingle in your loins as you wait for your STD test results . . . What a blast! But it's not all fun and Valtrex. Most of the time when you're single you just don't make the effort to cook a good meal for yourself. And that's what this chapter is all about: celebrating the single life with food! (Some people call this "emotional eating." *Pfft,* what do they know?)

When you're flying solo, it's super important to eat home-cooked meals because all that takeout will tax you. Before you know it, you'll be the one e-dating with an "artsy-emo" webcam pic because the wide shot ain't pretty. Even if your mom stocks your fridge once a week with cannelloni, that isn't a home-cooked meal—it's a salty bribe for grandchildren.

Now I know that cooking-for-one complaints are common: "Nobody is there to share it.""Nobody is there to chat.""I don't like hamsters." I hear you; but if you really think about it, who deserves a homemade feast more than you? Not only do you pay the bills, you're the only one who can give yourself an orgasm in under thirty seconds. 'Nuff said.

Being Single
IS ALL ABOUT YOU!

You call the shots!

You set the pace!

You die alone!

Crispy Salmon
with Leek Sauce

Salmon and singles have a lot in common. Salmon have to swim upstream hundreds of miles to spawn, singles have to surf through hundreds of crappy dating profiles. Salmon lower their temperature to mate, singles lower their standards. And at the end of the day, they both end up hot, sweaty, and covered in butter.

Servings: 2

LEEK SAUCE

- Warm a saucepan on medium-low. Add 1 tablespoon unsalted butter and sauté garlic clove until golden, about 2 minutes.
- Add leek and sauté until soft, about 5 minutes.
- Turn up the heat to medium. Add vegetable stock, minced parsley, a *small pinch of sea salt, and freshly cracked pepper. Let this simmer another 5 minutes.
- Discard garlic, add fresh dill, stir and set aside.

SALMON FILLETS

- Heat 1 tablespoon olive oil in a frying pan on medium heat. Add 1 tablespoon butter. (Butter has protein, which will make the salmon crispy.)
- Put the salmon fillets in the butter skin-side down and cook for about 5 to 8 minutes. Watch the salmon; when you see it's cooked halfway through, flip it over, and let it cook for another 1 to 3 minutes (until it's sufficiently cooked—or uncooked—to your liking.) Take it off the heat.

*SHKIAFFING IT TOGETHER

- Slap down a handful of raw baby spinach on a plate, slide the salmon fillet over the top, and spoon on lots of leek sauce. Squirt with fresh lemon juice and shkoff while surfing PerezHilton.com.

Grocery List

- Unsalted butter (2 tablespoons)
- Garlic (1 clove, degermed and crushed)
- Leek (½, thinly sliced)
- Vegetable stock (1 cup)
- Fresh flat-leaf parsley (*handful, minced)
- S&P
- Fresh dill (handful, finely chopped)
- Extra virgin olive oil (1 tablespoon)
- Salmon fillets with skin (2)
- Baby spinach (2 handfuls)
- Fresh lemons (2)

Gear

- Saucepan
- Large frying pan

Nadventure

ONLINE DATING:
Here's more proof that we're better off alone than in the company of "dogralf." These are all actual opening lines from real dating profiles. I left all spelling and grammatical errors intact . . .

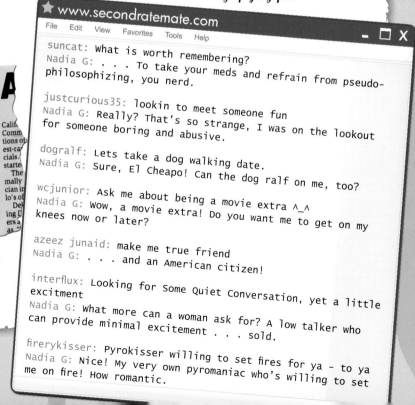

www.secondratemate.com

File   Edit   View   Favorites   Tools   Help

suncat: What is worth remembering?
Nadia G: . . . To take your meds and refrain from pseudo-philosophizing, you nerd.

justcurious35: lookin to meet someone fun
Nadia G: Really? That's so strange, I was on the lookout for someone boring and abusive.

dogralf: Lets take a dog walking date.
Nadia G: Sure, El Cheapo! Can the dog ralf on me, too?

wcjunior: Ask me about being a movie extra ^_^
Nadia G: Wow, a movie extra! Do you want me to get on my knees now or later?

azeez junaid: make me true friend
Nadia G: . . . and an American citizen!

interflux: Looking for Some Quiet Conversation, yet a little excitment
Nadia G: What more can a woman ask for? A low talker who can provide minimal excitement . . . sold.

firerykisser: Pyrokisser willing to set fires for ya - to ya
Nadia G: Nice! My very own pyromaniac who's willing to set me on fire! How romantic.

Mac & Cheese

Mac & Cheese is a staple of the single life. But while making Kraft Dinner out of a box can be a little depressing, this creamy homemade version will have you smiling that you don't have to share one bite. . . . Gawd that's cheesy.

Servings: 4

PASTA

- Boil fusilli pasta in salted water until half-cooked, about 6 to 7 minutes. (They'll finish cooking in the oven.) Strain and set aside.

SAUCE

- Heat a saucepan on medium. Add 1 tablespoon unsalted butter and minced onion. Sauté until onions soften, about 8 minutes.
- Add milk, half & half, and bay leaf. Bring mixture to a slow boil, then turn the heat to medium-low. Throw in the cheddar, Swiss, and Fontina cheeses, and freshly cracked pepper. Stir until melted, then taste. If it needs salt, add some.
- Remove bay leaf.

BAKING

- Preheat oven to 350°F. Grease a baking dish with 1 tablespoon of unsalted butter.
- In a big bowl combine pasta and sauce; mix to coat every noodle. Pour into a baking dish and sprinkle liberally with bread crumbs.
- Bake for 40 minutes.

SHKIAFFING IT TOGETHER

- There's nothing to shkiaff together, just grab a spoon and dig in!

Grocery List
- Fusilli pasta (450g package)
- Unsalted butter (2 tablespoons)
- Yellow onion (¼ cup, minced)
- Whole milk, 3.25% MF (1 cup)
- Half & half, 15% MF (1 cup)
- Bay leaf (1)
- Cheddar cheese, aged minimum 5 years (1 cup, grated)
- Swiss cheese (½ cup, grated)
- Fontina cheese (½ cup, grated)
- S&P
- Bread crumbs

Gear
- Large pot
- Saucepan
- Medium-sized baking dish
- Large mixing bowl

nadvice

Ladies, we all know the story: You and your girlfriends are dressed to kill and head to the club. After a couple of cocktails, you scan the room for some sexy prey. You spot a potential victim, but just as you're about to shoot him a killer-coy smile (or at least one of those smiles that you imagine to be killer-coy when you're tanked), you find yourself surrounded, yes, encircled by panting Losers. But when life gives you lemons, make lemonade . . . and get someone else to supply the tequila. See, Losers do have a use after all: free drinks.

By familiarizing yourself with the LOSER SPECIMEN GUIDE, you'll be able to distinguish between different species of Losers, scan their personalities for weak spots, and ultimately "fish" a drink from them in less than three minutes—about the same amount of time you'd spend telling them to take a hike, but with a better return on emotional investment. Onward.

LOSER SPECIMEN GUIDE

This guide uses a five-point rating system, five being the easiest to fish for drinks.

THE MEDITERRANEAN ♟ ♟ ♟ ♟ ♟

This Loser wears too much hair gel and sports fashion from the early 90s. He speaks with an overbearing Italian accent even though his family immigrated to North America eons ago. He always owns a business of sorts and offers you work in one of his "bars." The truth is, he's a Crisco Casanova that still lives with his parents, but he likes to flash his (dad's) cash, so . . .

He's the easiest to fish. When he starts talking, just smile and tell him flat out, "Hey, buy me drink." He'll do it, I promise. This type believes he's "the man," and "the man" must buy a lady a drink. Done. And off you go.

THE ARTIST/FILMMAKER ♟

This Loser hasn't created anything but a turd, but he acts as if he's some hotshot protégé. He wears dark clothing and has no tangible sense of style. He's usually skinny and smiles as if he's withholding a juicy secret. *Ma please!

This type is the most difficult to fish. The Artist considers himself a "neo–post modern man," so he feels that he owes you nothing—after all, his obnoxious tone is a gift in itself! You have to flat-out lie to get this twit to purchase some pilsner. Ask him to buy the first round and you'll get the second, and then top that off with "Isn't that film *Delicatessen* genius?!" Once the drinks arrive and you take one sip, you suddenly have to pee. End credits.

TACKY PARTY BOY ♟ ♟ ♟ ♟

Tacky Party Boy is loud and easily identifiable by his trendy, cheap clothing. This Loser is usually tall and always has an entourage of shorter, Lower-Level Losers worshipping him. He speaks of popular DJs and after-hours parties. He has A.D.D. and stares around the room wildly. He also can be seen doing the intense "air-punch" dance.

All you have to do is dance around a bit and say, "Man, I *love* deep house, where's the after-party?!" He'll tell you where it's at, then you say, "I'm *so* gonna be there, I can't wait! But its only midnight, let's get the party started right now! <enter giggles> You like shots?" Because he's easily excitable and eager to prove to his sycophantic friends who the Alpha Party Animal is, he'll *have* to buy the shots. Down 'em fast and you're off to the dance floor . . . at another club.

THE OLDER, OUT-OF-PLACE BUSINESSMAN ♟ ♟ ♟

He's the only one wearing a tie and thinks highly of himself because he's fourteen years older than everyone else in the club. Everything he "owns" he got on credit. This type played the market and lost everything in the tech stock crash. Since his life has crumbled and his wife left him, he's on the prowl and looking to impress nubile young minds with his corporate camouflage.

On one hand, chicken-hawkers are used to paying for attention, so this makes them an easy fish. On the other hand, they don't want to *feel* like their paying for attention, so you've got to make an effort to be subtle. Look bored and say, "I'm so tired of this scene, everyone is so *immature* . . . " Before he has time to respond, order two martinis and stare at him coquettishly, "So, what do you do?" Deal closed.

This guide covers the basics, but mind that there are so many types of Losers out there that it would be impossible to list them all . . . but they do have one thing in common—some money. So follow these simple guidelines and you'll never waste another minute (or dime) again. Remember: Why brush them off when you can shake them down? Cheers.

Perfect Spinach Salad
with Grilled Pears

In my book this is the perfect spinach salad—literally. It combines tangy, sweet, salty, and spicy flavors. Whenever you're making a salad, try to keep a balance of these four flavors in mind.

Servings: 1

DRESSING

- In a jar, combine canola oil, a few drops of toasted sesame oil, rice wine vinegar, brown sugar, soy sauce, Wasabi paste, and lots of freshly cracked pepper.
- Cover the jar and shake like hell to emulsify.

PEARS

- Heat the grill to high.
- Slice the Asian pears into ½-inch thick rings. Lightly brush the pears with maple syrup and grill for 1 to 2 minutes per side, until they get some good grill marks on them.

SHKIAFFING IT TOGETHER

- Throw the baby spinach, grilled pears, and scallions into a big bowl. Drizzle with dressing and top with chow mein noodles.

nadvice

This salad is also great with oranges, mangos, grilled chicken, or a male stripper.

Grocery List
- Canola oil (1 tablespoon)
- Toasted sesame oil
- Rice wine vinegar (1 tablespoon)
- Brown sugar (1 tablespoon)
- Soy sauce (1 tablespoon)
- Wasabi paste (½ tablespoon)
- Freshly cracked pepper
- Asian pears (2)
- Real maple syrup
- Baby spinach (3 cups)
- Scallions (handful, thinly sliced)
- Chow mein noodles

Gear
- Jar with lid
- Grill (If you don't have a grill, just slice up some fresh pears)
- Large mixing bowl

Yeah.

CHAPTER.2

One-Night-Stand Breakfasts

One-night stands may get a bad rap, but they're essential. If it weren't for the one-night stand, how would we know that binge drinking doesn't *reeeally* count as a shared hobby? How would we know that a big nose means nothing more than buddy needs a nose-job? And at the end of the day, if it weren't for the fruits of the one-night stand, most of us wouldn't be here reading, or writing, this chapter.

As awkward as it may be to feed a one-night stand, it's imperative to have breakfast with a new lover. It allows you to uncover the mysteries of his personality, like his hobbies . . . or his name. Breakfasts and one-night stands also have a lot in common: They're both easy, but the challenge lies in getting them out while they're still hot. So always start with the food that takes longest to cook.

Now granted, not every one-night stand deserves a good breakfast, but let's optimize: It's the morning after, and there's a gorgeous man sleeping in your bed . . . and unless you're a hungover straight guy, this is a good thing. So, let's get cooking.

The "Big" Breakfast:
Ham and Home Fries

This breakfast is reserved for prime catches only—the hotties that have *real* (three-month) relationship potential. As the old Italian saying goes: *Nothing says romance like big in the pants.* (Hey, I said the saying was old, not classy.)

Servings: 2

HOME FRIES

- Wash and peel the potatoes. Cut them in half lengthwise, then slice into ¼-inch pieces.
- Heat 2 tablespoons of canola oil in a large frying pan on medium heat. Sauté potato slices for about 10 minutes.
- Add in onion, garlic, a *big pinch of paprika, and small pinches of chile flakes, sea salt, and pepper. Mix the ingredients together and fry for another 8 minutes. In the last few minutes of cooking turn up the heat to medium-high and press down on the potatoes to crisp them up.
- Add fresh parsley and stir to coat the potatoes. Remove from heat and cover to keep warm.

HAM

- Now it's time for a sweet pork . . . side dish: Maple Ham.
- Heat a medium frying pan on medium-low. Add maple syrup and ham. Cook until warmed through, about 3 minutes.

SHKIAFFING IT TOGETHER

- Grab a big plate, add a ton of home fries, a slice of ham, drizzle with hot maple syrup. Serve with ketchup, OJ, and your e-mail address on a napkin.

Grocery List

- Potatoes (2)
- Canola oil
- Yellow onion (1, diced)
- Garlic (1 clove, degermed & minced)
- Paprika
- Crushed chile flakes
- S&P
- Fresh flat-leaf parsley (¼ cup, finely chopped)
- Real maple syrup (¼ cup)
- Thick-sliced Black Forest ham (2 slices)

Gear

- Large frying pan (preferably nonstick)
- Medium frying pan

nadvice

Remember to play safe! I don't have a recipe for Hepatitis Hash Browns. Although I do have one for Crab Cakes . . .

The "Small" Breakfast:

Smoked Salmon
& Hollandaise

This breakfast may not be huge, but always remember that a smaller offering can compensate by being rich. **Warning:** You may be shocked when you see how much butter is needed to make a hollandaise sauce, but man is it ever good.

Servings: 2

SIMPLE HOLLANDAISE

- Heat a saucepan on medium-low and melt ½ cup of butter in it. Set aside.
- In a food processor, combine 4 egg yolks, juice of ½ a fresh lemon, a big pinch of dry mustard, big pinch of paprika, and small pinches of sea salt and freshly cracked pepper. Blend for a few seconds.
- Reheat the melted butter on medium until it just starts to sputter but not burn. Pour the melted butter into a gravy boat.
- Turn the food processor back on, and slowly add the hot butter. (Pour the butter in a slow, thin stream; if you dump in the hot butter too quickly, you'll cook the eggs and end up with a curdled sauce.)
- Once this is done, remove food processor bowl and add chopped drained capers and lots of minced fresh dill; mix and then set aside.

THE BAGEL

- Heat a frying pan on medium. Add 1 teaspoon of butter and coat the bottom of the pan with it.
- Slice a fresh bagel in half. Place the bagel slices in the pan and crack an egg into the middle of each bagel hole. Cook for about 3 minutes. Flip it over and cook for 2 minutes more.

SHKIAFFING IT TOGETHER

- Place the egg-bagel in the center of a plate, top with wild smoked salmon, and spoon on a generous amount of hollandaise. Sprinkle with chives.

Grocery List
- Unsalted butter (½ cup and 1 teaspoon)
- Eggs (6)
- Fresh lemon (1)
- Dry mustard
- Paprika
- S&P
- Capers (1 tablespoon, chopped and drained)
- Fresh dill (1 bunch, minced)
- Bagel (1)
- Wild smoked salmon (4 thick slices)
- Chives (1 bunch)

Gear
- Saucepan
- Food processor
- Gravy boat (or anything that has a pouring lip)
- Frying pan

*Bro, when it comes to choosing good salmon, smoked or not, you wanna make sure dat da flesh is fresh, slick, and firm. Dat's why you always gotta go wit da wild stuff. I don't want to be a snob, but most salmon is mass-farmed, bro. Dat means dat deez fish grow up in pools so cramped togedder dat day can't move. Der muscles are atrophied, bro, atrophied! And dat's not all: Because deez fish are fed garbage dey have to be freakin' dyed pink to fake a natural salmon color! Unacceptable, bro.

The "Quick" Breakfast:
Orange Salad & a Mocha

Where I come from we do not buy fancy salt. We flavor our food the old fashioned way, with tears. So when Nadia told me to review gourmet salts I was very uncomfortable … then I realized I had forgotten to remove the nipple clamps. Here we go!

This breakfast is reserved for the *scragglers, the ones you want out fast. Why make them breakfast in the first place? Two words: *camera phone.* The last thing you need is to be buddy's vengeful Facebook trophy, so play it smooth.

Servings: 2

BLOOD ORANGE SALAD

- Peel blood oranges, separate into wedges, slice into bits, and place in a bowl. Drizzle with 1 to 2 tablespoons olive oil. Sprinkle with a small pinch of black lava salt. Mix to coat and set aside.

MOCHA

- Into a jar throw cocoa powder, brown sugar, and ¼ cup milk. Seal the jar and shake vigorously (approximately 1 to 2 minutes) until the liquid is smooth and there are no powdery cocoa balls floating around.
- Heat a small saucepan on medium-low. Add ¾ cup milk and the cocoa mixture. Stir and warm through. Don't boil.
- Add two shots of espresso to each drinking bowl. Pour in the hot chocolate and sprinkle with cocoa powder (because you're fancy like that.)

SHKIAFFING IT TOGETHER

- Place the blood orange salad on one side of a large plate and top with toasted baguette slices (to sop up all of that precious orange oil). Place the mocha drinking bowl on the other side. Serve with a plastic smile and an urgent dentist appointment.

Grocery List
- Blood oranges (4)
- Extra virgin olive oil
- Black lava salt
- Cocoa powder (2 tablespoons)
- Brown sugar (2 heaping tablespoons)
- Whole milk, 3.25% MF (1 cup)
- Espresso coffee (4 shots)
- Crusty baguette (1)

Gear
- Mixing bowl
- Small jar
- Saucepan
- Drinking bowls (2)

CYPRUS BLACK LAVA SALT
Cyprus black lava salt is Mediterranean flake salt mixed with activated charcoal. The charcoal makes for a dramatic color and a mineral flavor. It also cleanses the body. But let it be known that no matter how much you sprinkle on, it will never, never, get rid of that dirty feeling deep inside.

Use it for simple salads, fish, foie gras, and spice rubs!

PINK HIMALAYAN SALT
This tangy salt is made from crystals that were formed millions of years ago deep in the earth. The Himalayans use it for trading, and some even believe it has magical powers … But ever since I was bitten by a leprechaun I no longer believe in magic. A piece of me died that day.

It is perfect on sushi, carpaccio, and mild aged cheeses.

FLEUR DE SEL
Fleur de sel is a delicate sea salt with a surprising delicately salty flavor. It is made from hand-harvesting "young" crystals from evaporating sea water in France.

It brings out the best in caramel and chocolate desserts.

CHAPTER.3

Anxiety Blasters

Anxiety is the plague of the Net Generation, kind of like smallpox, but more panicked and less itchy. Anxiety is no fun: the pressure on your chest, the sinking feeling in your stomach, the voices in your head that tell you to "Kill! Kill! Kill!" Nope, no fun at all.

I remember my first panic attack as clearly as the day I lost my virginity (okay, maybe a little clearer). There I was, eight years old, watching *Spaceballs,* when all of a sudden *tsaketa* my heart starts palpitating wildly; the room implodes into blackness; speedy visions of fleshy, skinless creatures hijack my mind. They move so quickly! Their bloody, twitching muscles hurrying, rushing, skipping frames . . . hundreds of choppy, bleeding creatures, scuttling to get things done! But what things? *WHAT THINGS?!!*

Ahem.

These days a variety of things will trigger a panic attack: phone calls over twenty-six seconds, cotton balls, small children. . . . I know what you're thinking, "That's so sad, Nadia G will never experience the joy of holding a small cotton ball." Silence. I've accepted it.

Although there's no cure for anxiety, there *are* ways to alleviate the suffering. Social isolation, rabid outbursts, and mentally pummeling yourself into a fetal position are some of my favorite techniques. Robust meals will also help, because there's nothing like a belly full of carbs to just knock you the fuck out.

Okay! So, if you're dealing with anxiety, this chapter is for you! These recipes will soothe your shriveled soul, plus they practically make themselves, so you can spend even more time in front of your computer researching lung disease. . . . On to the recipes.

For the longest time I suspected my panic attacks were due to rockin' too hard, so I cleaned up my act, and *surprise surprise* . . .
Life still sucks!

Nonna's Potato Croquettes

This recipe comes from my paternal grandmother, Nonna Teresa. When I was a kid I'd go nuts over these croquettes! But there was a downside. To eat them I had to go over to her house, and her living room used to creep me out. She had these "decorative" rubber lizards everywhere, their mouths filled with little, sharp, plastic teeth. As a young girl I didn't really know what to make of the lizards. Hell, I *still* don't know what to make of those lizards.

Servings: 4

POTATO MIXTURE

- Slice potatoes into chunks. Place them in a large pot of salted water, boil about 15 minutes until fork-tender, and then drain.
- In a frying pan, heat 1 teaspoon of olive oil on medium heat. Add garlic clove and sauté 2 minutes until golden. Set aside.
- In a big bowl combine the cooked potatoes with grated parmesan, the sautéed garlic and the oil from the pan, parsley, a small pinch of sea salt, and freshly cracked pepper. Roughly mash it all together and let cool in the fridge for 30 minutes to 1 hour.

SHKIAFFING IT TOGETHER

- Once the mash has cooled, roll a bunch of croquettes into any shape you like. (I usually roll them up into ½-inch thick fingers.)
- Beat the eggs in a bowl. Dip the croquettes in the eggs and then coat/roll them in the Italian-seasoned bread crumbs.
- In a large frying pan, heat ¼-inch of olive oil over medium heat. Throw in a small pinch of bread crumbs to test the temperature. When the tester crumbs start sizzling fast, it's time to get cracking.
- Gently place the croquettes in the oil. Roll them around for a few seconds until the breadcrumbs are golden all over, and they're done.
- Place the fried croquettes on a paper towel to get rid of excess oil and shkoff immediately until placated.

Grocery List
- Russet potatoes (4, large)
- Garlic (1 clove, degermed and minced)
- Extra virgin olive oil (1 teaspoon plus more for frying)
- Parmigiano Reggiano (½ cup, grated)
- Fresh flat-leaf parsley (½ cup, minced)
- S&P
- Eggs (3)
- Italian-seasoned bread crumbs

Gear
- Large pot
- Medium-sized frying pan
- Large mixing bowl
- Large frying pan

Fun Facts

Did you know that the carbohydrates in potatoes act as a tranquilizer by increasing the amount of serotonin in your brain . . . and that I used to dissect live ants when I was six years old?

Spaghetti alla Puttanesca

Spaghetti alla Puttanesca means "spaghetti the way a whore would make it." Let me explain . . .

Back in the 1950s, Italy was rife with legal brothels. To prevent squabbles between the housewives and hos (hey, this was before reality TV), the prostitutes were only allowed to shop at the local market once a week, so whatever they bought had to last. That's why this recipe is made up of preserves . . . and slutty goodness. Preserves not only prevent virgin/whore beat downs, but they also cater to the anxiety-ridden agoraphobic in you! Good times.

Servings: 4

SHKIAFFING IT TOGETHER

- Boil spaghetti in salted water until *almost* al dente (about 8 minutes). The pasta will finish cooking in the sauce. Strain.
- Cut cherry tomatoes in half. Mash 6 anchovy fillets with a fork. Roughly chop capers. Pit and chop the kalamata olives. Degerm and mince garlic. Set ingredients aside.
- Heat a large pan on medium and add olive oil, minced garlic, and a small pinch of hot chile flakes. Fry garlic for 2 minutes until golden.
- Add mashed anchovy fillets. Stir and sauté for 30 seconds.
- Throw in the cherry tomatoes. Turn the heat down to medium-low, stir and sauté for about 10 more minutes, until tomatoes begin to create a light sauce. Then add chopped capers, 1 heaping tablespoon chopped kalamata olives, a small pinch of brown sugar, a small pinch of sea salt if needed (usually this sauce is salty enough because of the anchovies), and freshly cracked pepper to taste. Stir.
- Add the strained pasta to the sauce.
- Sprinkle pasta with a small pinch of fresh minced parsley. Mix well with tongs until pasta finishes cooking al dente, about 5 more minutes.

Grocery List
- Spaghetti (1 package, 450g)
- Sweet cherry tomatoes (26)
- Anchovy fillets (1 can)
- Capers (1 heaping tablespoon)
- Kalamata olives (10)
- Garlic (1 clove)
- Extra virgin olive oil (4 tablespoons)
- Hot chile flakes
- Brown sugar
- S&P
- Fresh flat-leaf parsley

Gear
- Big pot
- Large pan
- Tongs

Bro, anchovies and olive oil are amazing sources of omega-3 fatty acids—total anxiety fighters! Dey give anxiety a beating, bro! BOOM! Right in da *teet!

23

Lentil & Caramelized Onion Soup

Lentils are rich in folic acid, and diets lacking in folic acid contribute to anxiety. That's why when you're panicking there's nothing like the comforting warmth of lentils. They're like a hug from a unicorn on a starlit beach in heaven.

This recipe isn't exactly quick, but when you're freaking out it helps to stay busy and keep your mind off of that strange growth near your armpit. *(Is it cancerous? Are you sick? Because if you're sick you'll lose your job, and if you lose your job, you can't pay your bills, and if you can't pay your bills, you'll end up homeless, and if you're homeless, no one will ever love you, and if no one loves you, you'll die alone . . . stinky and alone . . . all because of that growth . . . or zit.)*

Servings: 4–6

CROUTONS

- Preheat oven at 350°F.
- Slice baguette into 1-inch cubes. Degerm and mince garlic. In a jar combine the garlic and 3 tablespoons olive oil; cover and shake well.
- Brush garlic-olive oil on all sides of the bread cubes. Place bread cubes on a baking sheet and bake 20 to 25 minutes, until crispy and crunchy.

CARAMELIZED ONIONS

- Place a large soup pot over medium heat and add 3 tablespoons olive oil, red onion slices, and a small pinch of sea salt. Stir to separate rings and coat with oil.
- Once the onions become translucent, turn the heat down to medium-low and caramelize the onions by sautéing them for 30 minutes, stirring often so all sides get browned. Don't skimp on the caramelization—be patient. You'll know they're done once they're reduced to half their original size and are dark brown, very soft, and sweet.

OPERATION: CARAMELIZED ONIONS
00:00 Calling BlackEagle. Too many onions in the pan. I don't think we'll make it.
00:15 Onions are breaking down from our assault. They're showing weakness, stringiness. I am hopeful.
00:25 It is an onion massacre down here. All that was white is now a hazy brown. My hands are sticky with the sugars of onion blood. WHY GOD? WHY?! Drowsiness is setting in.
00:35 BlackEagle, the mission is complete. Onion population has been reduced to half. I hope you are satisfied. Everything is dark, so dark . . . Ooh! Is that cognac?

- Deglaze the pot with the dry red wine. Add beef stock, a big pinch of thyme, and a bay leaf. Stir and simmer for 30 minutes.
- Then add cognac, rinsed lentils, and a small pinch of sea salt and freshly cracked pepper. Remove bay leaf and simmer for 5 more minutes.

SHKIAFFING IT TOGETHER

- Ladle the soup into 4 stoneware bowls. Top each with a layer of croutons and sprinkle with lots of grated Gruyère cheese. Broil in the oven until the cheese is golden brown and bubbling, about 10 minutes.

CHAPTER . 4

Furious Foods

*M*y grandmother used to say, "Life is like a big ventilator . . . that keeps sucking air into your shriveled lungs, while they stab your liver with forks!" . . . I miss you Nonna, RIP.

She had a point, though. Some days just suck. Maybe your computer crashed, or maybe that rash *isn't* ingrown hair . . . Whatever the case may be, there are ways to cope. Some people like to go for a jog, others turn to yoga. Me? I like to break things and take it out on my loved ones. To each her own.

Sometimes you're so pissed that you get that pulsing, whining feeling in your groin, Angry Wuss. Ladies, you know what I'm talking about: the feeling that makes you simultaneously want to punch *and* hump something. If you don't know what I'm talking about, let me take you down memory lane. You're four years old, strapped into a rigid snowsuit, your underpants are giving you a serious wedgie under ten layers of clothing, you're sweating, waiting in an overheated house. . . . *Now that's Angry Wuss.*

But it's no wonder we lose it sometimes. We live in a world that assaults us on a daily basis! Even in the comfort of our own living room, BOOM!, those shameless Viagra commercials come on. Seriously, if you're too old and out of shape to get it up, nature probably intended it to stay down. And if your saggy, hairy ass is getting some, I don't wanna hear about it! Gawd!

Anyways, if you've had a horrible day, these hot and spicy dishes will pair perfectly with your *whine*. Tsaketa. Let's get cooking.

nadvice

Don't spend too much energy harping on a crappy situation. Remember: Tomorrow is another day . . . filled with even more stress and letdowns!

Pissed Penne Arrabiata

When you're hot, sometimes life can be frustrating because people always want to touch you. "Come here Hans," they say. "Let me touch you." When this happens don't get mad, just tell them firmly "No. I don't want to be touched right now." Then find a quiet corner and breathe. Just breathe in and out. You'll feel better.

In case you didn't already know, *arrabiata* is Italian for "angry." So is keying your ex's car, but we won't go there. Arrabiata is also a fresh tomato sauce with lots of "angry" hot peppers that'll transfer the pain in a good way. Just be careful when you're handling chiles—always wash your hands or somebody could get hurt . . . unless you're pissed at your lover. Then don't.

Servings: 4

TOMATO SAUCE

- In a large frying pan heat olive oil over medium heat. Add crushed garlic and red chile pepper. Sauté for 3 to 4 minutes.
- Pour a can of *San Marzano tomatoes into a large bowl and crush them with your bare hands. Pour tomatoes into the frying pan, stir, then add torn basil leaves, a big pinch brown sugar, a small pinch of sea salt, and freshly cracked pepper to taste. Simmer for 10 minutes.

PASTA

- Bring a pot of salted water to a boil, add penne and boil until almost al dente. (It'll finish cooking in the sauce.) Strain.

SHKIAFFING IT TOGETHER

- Pour the pasta into the tomato sauce, and mix for a few minutes using tongs. Plop a portion on a plate and shkoff with a vengeance . . . or lots of freshly grated parmesan.

Grocery List

- Extra virgin olive oil (2 tablespoons)
- Garlic (2 cloves, degermed and crushed)
- Red chile pepper (1–2, thinly sliced)
- Whole San Marzano tomatoes (796ml can)
- Fresh basil (4–5 leaves)
- Brown sugar
- S&P
- Penne rigate (500g)
- Parmigiano Reggiano

Gear

- Large frying pan
- Large mixing bowl
- Large pot
- Tongs

nadvice

You know what pisses me off? Tomatoes. These days they have less fucking flavor than "punk rock" and started going to shit at about the same time. Even cherry tomatoes suck now! The only way to get a great tomato is to grow your own, but a can of San Marzano comes close . . .

Chili Con Carnage

nadvice

When you're served a shiny cac cherry on this poop sundae called life, let it out! Scream, cry, attack your Rachael Ray voodoo doll! There's nothing worse than keeping it in . . . except maybe e-mailing it out in ALL CAPS.

You know what else pisses me off? Low-rise jeans. Listen up jean designers out there: As a grown woman I do not feel "sexy" with my underpants hanging out of my jeans, I feel sloppy. Now it may come as a surprise to you, but I also don't enjoy worrying about exposing my ass every time I sit down. Weird, isn't it? I know you've tried to remedy the problem by designing "fashion-forward" high-waisted pantaloons, but for some reason it feels a little forced when I'm out to buy milk and my belt-line is scraping the bottom of my fucking bra!!!

Gawd! Can someone please design a pair of jeans that are normal?! Pfft. Let's make some chili.

Servings: 4–6

CHILES

- Fill two mixing bowls with water. Add Ancho chile to one bowl and Chipotle chile to the other. Let them plump up for a few hours.
- Chop the plumped-up chipotle and ancho chiles. Mince the jalapeno pepper. Set aside.

CHILI SAUCE

- Heat a large saucepan over medium heat. Add bacon and fry until crisp. Remove bacon, set it aside, and keep the grease in the pan.
- Fry garlic in bacon grease for 2 minutes until golden. Then add minced jalapeno, chopped chipotle and ancho chiles, onion, and sweet green pepper. Sauté for 10 minutes.
- Crush the San Marzano tomatoes (by hand) and add them to the peppers along with a small pinch of chili powder, big pinches of cumin, Greek oregano, and brown sugar, and a small pinch of sea salt and freshly cracked pepper to taste. Simmer on medium-low heat.

MEAT

- Heat olive oil in a large frying pan over medium heat. Add organic ground beef and a small pinch of sea salt and freshly cracked pepper to taste. Fry until cooked, about 10 minutes, then turn the heat to high and crisp up the meat for 2 more minutes.
- Add meat to the chili sauce and stir to mix thoroughly.
- Simmer chili, covered, for 1 hour. Every 15 minutes or so, give the chili some love and stir. In the last 10 minutes of cooking, add black beans. Stir.

SHKIAFFING IT TOGETHER

- Ladle some chili into a bowl. Add a big pinch of fresh, minced cilantro and a handful of finely chopped scallion greens. Sprinkle with coarsely grated aged cheddar cheese. Shkoff with whole wheat tortilla chips or soft tacos and sour cream.

Grocery List

- Dried ancho chile (1)
- Dried chipotle pepper (1)
- Jalapeno pepper (1)
- Canadian bacon (5 slices)
- Garlic (2 cloves, degermed and crushed)
- Large onion (1, chopped)
- Sweet green pepper (1, chopped)
- Whole San Marzano tomatoes (796ml can)
- Chili powder
- Cumin
- Greek oregano
- Brown sugar
- S&P
- Extra virgin olive oil (2 tablespoons)
- Lean organic ground beef (1½ pounds)
- Black beans (450g can)
- Fresh cilantro (1 bunch)
- Scallions (1 bunch)
- Aged cheddar cheese, minimum 5 years old (½ cup)
- Whole wheat tortilla chips

Gear

- 2 medium-sized mixing bowls
- Large saucepan with a lid
- Large frying pan

Chile Raspberry Parfait

I bet you didn't know that "Stressed" is "Desserts" spelled backwards. That's all the intro you need, baby. Now go buy some whipping cream.

Servings: 2

SPICY SAUCE

- In a food processor combine 1 cup fresh raspberries, chile pepper, and 1 heaping tablespoon brown sugar (or to taste). Puree and set aside.

CREAM

- In a clean food processor cup combine whipping cream, dark rum, 1 tablespoon brown sugar, and the seeds of ½ a vanilla bean. Whip until peaks form.

WALNUTS

- Put 1 cup toasted walnuts in a ziplock bag, place the bag on your cutting board and roughly smash them with a can or something. Don't pulverize, we want chunks. (Instructions on toasting nuts on page 77.)
- Place crumbled walnuts in a mixing bowl and add honey and a pinch of sea salt. Mix well.

SHKIAFFING IT TOGETHER

- To a large martini glass add 1 tablespoon honey-walnut mixture and press down to settle. Then add a layer of fresh raspberries, a tablespoon of the spicy raspberry puree, and a layer of whipped cream. Repeat layers until the glass is full and top it off with a sprig of fresh mint.

Grocery List

- Fresh raspberries (2 cups)
- Red hot chile pepper (1, roughly chopped with stem removed)
- Brown sugar (2 tablespoons)
- Whipping cream (1 cup)
- Fine dark rum (1 tablespoon)
- Vanilla bean (1)
- Toasted walnuts (1 cup)
- Honey (1 tablespoon)
- Sea salt
- Fresh mint (2 sprigs)

Gear

- Food processor
- Some blunt object to smash nuts (that sounds worse than it really is)
- Small mixing bowl
- 2 large martini glasses

> When I was a child I suffered many beatings.

CHAPTER. 5

BAG 'EM TAG 'EM MEALS

I'm a hopeless romantic. I believe that there's love out there for everyone . . . who's good-looking. And if you're lucky enough to meet that special someone, you've got to make sure that they don't get away! But since chloroform is illegal, harsh on the palate, and *surprisingly expensive,* this chapter is devoted to a culinary approach.

You know you got it bad when you spend eight hours on a "casual" e-mail, or you Photoshop pics to see what your kids would look like (so what if Junior looks like an angry mongoose, he's yours and that's what matters!). You've even stalked them online to the point that Google sent you a restraining order. If you have any of these symptoms, it's time to go in for the kill, or make 'em a home-cooked meal . . . semantics.

Now I warn you: The following meals are potent, and you should only serve them if you're 100 percent sure that this person's "the one" (for a while).

nadvice

When assessing if they're "the one," never mind lengthy discussions about values or goals; that takes too much energy! The surest way to know if you've got a keeper is to sniff their armpit. Oh, I'm serious. Take a nice big whiff. If you love what you smell, BINGO! If it stinks, chances are their genes are nastier than a pair of low-rises on Grandma.

LOCK DOWN FRENCH TOAST

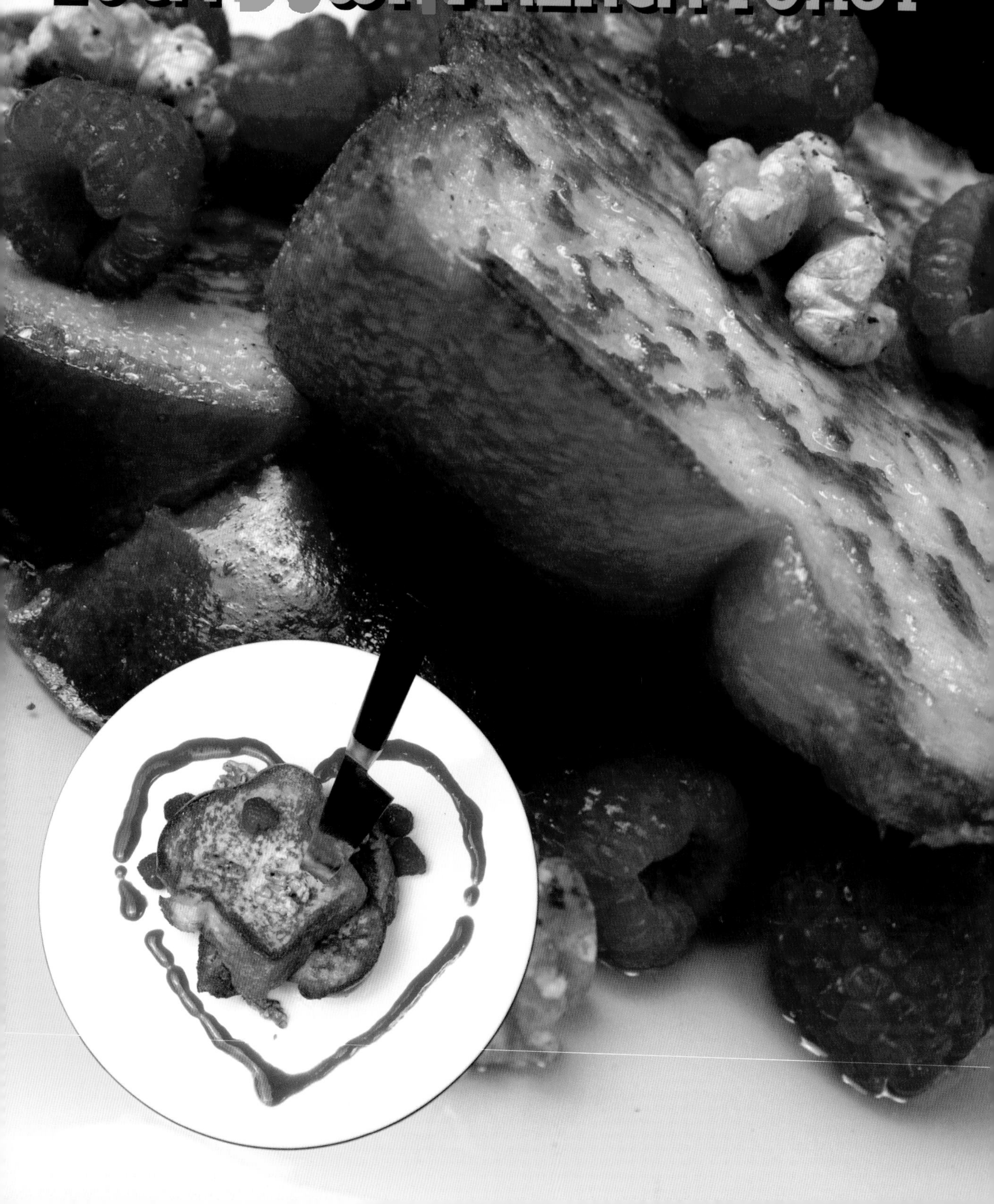

Lock Down French Toast is all about choosing the right bread—one that complements your lover's personality. If they're athletic, use multigrain. Head over heels for an artist? A flaky-ass croissant is an excellent choice. In the groove with a hippie? A violent baguette beating is the only friggin' answer.

Servings: 2

EGG MIXTURE

- In a bowl beat together eggs, the seeds of ½ a vanilla bean (slice the bean open length-wise and scrape out the seeds with your knife), a big pinch of brown sugar, a splash of milk, and a small pinch of salt.
- Slice 4 pieces of bread 1-inch thick. Drown in egg mixture.

BREAD

- Melt 1 tablespoon of butter in a large pan on medium heat. Fry bread until golden brown on both sides (about 3 to 5 minutes per side).

SHKIAFFING IT TOGETHER

- Grab a nice big plate and pile the French toast high. Throw on a bunch of fresh raspberries, some toasted walnuts, and serve with a shot glass of maple syrup.

You want your presentation to be simple and slick. See, you've already compromised your cool by serving breakfast in bed, so don't get too cutesy or they'll run for the door. No flowers, no heart-shaped syrup trails, and definitely no I LOVE YOU scrawled in strawberry juice with a big knife stabbed into the heart of it. Trust me: That one just doesn't work.

Grocery List

- Eggs (4)
- Vanilla bean (1)
- Brown sugar
- Milk (¼ cup)
- Sea salt
- Bread of your choice (4 thick slices)
- Unsalted butter (1 tablespoon)
- Raspberries (1 cup)
- Toasted walnuts (½ cup)
- Maple syrup

Gear

- Medium-sized mixing bowl
- Large frying pan

nadvice

If this breakfast doesn't get 'em hooked, screw 'em! They're not worth the syrup! (Or at least that's what my editor wants me to say, Chubs.)

mom's CHICKEN SOUP

People just can't resist someone who makes them homemade chicken soup. Subconsciously, it reminds them of everything that's safe and good in the world (even if you're neither). At the first sign of a sniffle, cook up a hearty pot of Mom's Chicken Soup for your loved one, and consider it game over.

Servings: 4–6

CHICKEN STOCK

- In a stockpot, heat olive oil on medium heat. Add garlic cloves and sauté for 2 minutes until golden.
- Add onion and sauté for 8 minutes, until onions are translucent.
- Hack the whole chicken into pieces to expose the bones. Throw chicken pieces into the stockpot along with additional chicken bones.
- Add celery ribs and carrots and cover the massacre with water.
- Drop in chopped celery leaves and parsley. Let simmer, covered, on medium-low heat for a minimum of 3 hours.
- Strain the broth through a cheesecloth to remove all the nasty bits: the skin, the bones, the scum . . . especially the skin. (The skin is the worst . . . the way it floats around like that.)
- Reserve good chicken meat, discard everything else in the cheesecloth.
- Refrigerate broth overnight. The next day, remove solidified fat.

At this point you've got bona fide homemade chicken stock, aka liquid gold. You can choose to use it all for this chicken soup, or freeze a portion for future use. This recipe yields about 6 cups of stock.

CHICKEN SOUP

- Pour the broth into a pot and add whatever you want. I like to use potatoes, carrots, hand-picked chicken meat, and sea salt and freshly cracked pepper to taste.
- Simmer for another 30 minutes, until the vegetables are fork-tender.

Grocery List

- Extra virgin olive oil (3 tablespoons)
- Garlic (6 cloves, crushed & degermed)
- Large red onions (2, chopped)
- Whole chicken (gutted)
- Chicken bones (1 pound)
- Celery ribs (3, quartered)
- Carrots (3, quartered)
- Celery leaves (½ cup, chopped)
- Fresh flat-leaf parsley (½ cup, chopped)
- New potatoes (halved)
- Carrots (halved)
- Chicken meat (hand-picked)
- S&P

Gear

- Large stock pot
- Cheesecloth

nadvice

If you want to get fancy, quickly stir in a beaten egg during the last minute of simmering, using a fork. This will make a "Stracciatella" soup. (Italian egg-drop soup.)

FETTUCCINE ROSE
WITH SHRIMP

I credit my Mom for this recipe. She would only make it on special occasions and had my whole family addicted to it. My aunts and cousins would call at least two times a week begging and bartering family gossip just to get another hit.

Servings: 4

SAUCE

- Heat 2 tablespoons unsalted butter in a saucepan on medium heat. Add garlic and sauté for 2 minutes until golden.
- Add cherry tomatoes, and a small pinch each of the hot chile flakes, salt, and brown sugar. Sauté the tomatoes until they get soft and release their juice, about 5 to 8 minutes.
- Then add half & half and fresh parsley. Bring mixture to a slow boil over medium heat; the second it starts to boil, turn down heat to medium-low.
- Throw in tiger shrimp, 2 heaping tablespoons of freshly grated parmesan, and sea salt and freshly cracked pepper to taste (be careful with the salt, Parmesan is already very salty.)
- Stir and simmer for 5 more minutes, then take off the heat.

SHKIAFFING IT TOGETHER

- Boil some egg-based fettuccine in salted water until al dente. Strain and dump into a large mixing bowl. Add a ladleful of sauce, mix to coat. Top plated portions of pasta with 2 to 3 tablespoons of sauce and some shrimp. Serve with lots of freshly grated Parmesan.

Grocery List

- **Unsalted butter** (2 tablespoons)
- **Garlic** (1 clove, degermed and minced)
- **Sweet cherry tomatoes** (20, sliced in half)
- **Hot chile flakes**
- **S&P**
- **Brown sugar**
- **Half & half, 15% MF** (2 cups)
- **Fresh flat-leaf parsley** (handful, finely chopped)
- **Jumbo tiger shrimp** (10, deveined)
- **Parmigiano Reggiano** (freshly grated, ¼ cup)
- **Egg-based fettuccine** (500g)

Gear

- **Saucepan**
- **Large pot**
- **Large mixing bowl**

DEVEINING SHRIMP WIT PANOS

Bro, it's too easy to devein a shrimp. First you peel it, but leave da tail. Den you use a sharp paring knife to slice a ½-inch-deep cut into da back of da shrimp, from da tail to da tip. And finally, you remove da cac inside, bro. All da cac.

Nadventure

I once received an interesting comment about this recipe. It read: "Pfft. No real Italian would ever use cheese with seafood!" I promptly suggested an alternative: "Dear sir, you can always replace the Parmesan with a light sprinkling of 'Go Fuck Yourself.'" Hey, I'm all about options.

CHAPTER.6

Impress the In-laws

You may be expecting a bunch of clichéd, disparaging remarks about in-laws in this chapter, but personally, I've never had a problem with them. Then again, I've dated a lot of "Johnny Blenders" who wear more mascara than I do, so I think these parents were just happy that their son was dating a chick. Anyway, meeting your lover's parents for the first time is always uncomfortable, so here are a few tricks to help ease the pain . . .

- **Invite them over to *your* place for dinner.** Get your in-laws out of their comfort zone and onto your turf. By playing the gracious hostess you're in a position of power, and as guests they can't badger you.

- **Bamboozle them with a succulent meal.** See, you may think your in-laws are difficult, but subconsciously parents only care about one thing: whether their children are eating enough. My mom calls me at least once a day asking, "Did you eat? . . . When did you eat? . . . What did you eat? . . . Are you sure you ate? . . . When are you coming over to eat? . . . Nadia, I never see you no more, why you abandon the family?!" Good Gawd, Ma! The point is: This meal will prove that their precious baby is getting fed.

- **Pair an exquisite wine with each course.** Not only does this show class, it also shows them the door, as they tiredly down bottle number three, placated and happily stuffed. (You may want to disregard this step if self-control isn't your forte and you have a tendency to tell this "*really* funny joke about a nun, two sheep, and a horny bus driver.")

In the next few pages I'll dish out a dazzling three-course dinner and *Hans will give you the goods on rare organic wines that'll surprise. No really, the fact that he can describe these wines surprises me. So hide your "toys," mop that floor, and go all out with this meal because the earlier you suck in your in-laws, the better. Seriously, it's imperative to win them over because their disapproval could totally sabotage your relationship. My mom has given many a boyfriend the evil eye, and that seed of doubt opens a pandora's box that ultimately ends with Johnny Blender getting the boot. Plus, once you're "in" you'll forever benefit from *all kinds of precious family stuff, like free babysitting, weekly care packages . . . and their inheritance.

Time to lay it on thick...

Candied Pecan & Strawberry Salad

FIUMESECCU ROSE 2006

Rose wines are like men, if they're too sweet there's something wrong. Fiumeseccu Rose is a perfectly balanced aperitif wine. It has a sexy orange tinge and smells like mandarins and red berries.... On the flip-side it's also dry to the bone, has bite, and a down-to-earth finish. This wine is definitely marriage material.

Round 1: Distraction

This punchy mix of bright red berries, crunchy sweet pecans, and tart white balsamic will stave off weather-related niceties for at least another fifteen minutes, guaranteed.

Servings: 4

CANDIED PECANS

- Preheat oven to 300°F. Line a baking sheet with parchment paper.
- In a medium-sized mixing bowl beat 2 egg whites. Then add raw pecans, ¼ cup brown sugar, and sea salt. Mix with your hands until all pecans are evenly coated.
- Arrange pecans in a single layer on the baking sheet and bake for 30 minutes. Cool on a wire rack.

DRESSING

- Into a jar add olive oil, balsamic, 1 heaping teaspoon brown sugar, and a small pinch of sea salt and freshly cracked white pepper. Close lid and shake until thick.

SHKIAFFING IT TOGETHER

- In a big bowl combine mesclun greens, strawberries, and 4 tablespoons of the dressing. Mix well to coat.
- Place a cup of salad in the center of each plate. Throw on a generous handful of candied pecans. If you want to get really fancy, puree some strawberries with a big pinch of brown sugar and dot the side of the plate with it. Serve with a glass of crisp Rose wine.

Grocery List

- Eggs (2)
- Raw pecans (2 cups)
- Brown sugar (¼ cup plus 1 heaping teaspoon)
- Sea salt (½ tablespoon plus a pinch)
- Extra virgin olive oil (3 tablespoons)
- White balsamic vinegar, aged minimum 7 years (2 tablespoons)
- Freshly cracked white peppercorns
- Mesclun greens (6 cups)
- Strawberries (halved, 2 cups)
- Crisp Rose wine (pompous recommendation: Fiumeseccu Rose 2006.)

Gear

- Parchment paper
- Baking sheet
- Medium mixing bowl
- Wire rack
- Jar with lid
- Large mixing bowl

White peppercorns mock me—always so happy, so carefree. Bastards. If only I was allowed the luxury to ripen fully on the vine until I was ready. But no, not for *Yeheskel! I am always the black peppercorn, ripped away too young and green, then left to die in the scorching sun until I shrivel to blackness. HA! Let me tell you this Mr. White Peppercorn: You may be hotter on the tongue, but you will never be as aromatic as your dark brother! Only suffering can give you that extra flavor, and the sheltered life you have led will forever blind you to the beauty found only in hardship. Die white peppercorn. Die.

Gorgonzola & Portobello Farfalle

Round 2: Sedation

This creamy, earthy pasta will have your in-laws asking for seconds . . . but a second helping of a dish this rich will put them in a carb-induced coma. Bring it on.

Servings: 4

MUSHROOMS

- Heat butter in a frying pan on medium heat, then add Portobello mushrooms, garlic, and a small pinch of sea salt and freshly cracked white pepper. Sauté for 10 minutes, discard garlic, strain juice, and set aside.

GORGONZOLA SAUCE

- Heat a large saucepan on medium and add half & half, Gorgonzola, a small pinch of sea salt, and freshly cracked white pepper to taste. Stir until cheese melts and sauce begins to simmer, about 10 minutes.
- Lower the heat, delicately spoon in the 'shrooms, and stir twice—no more! You don't want to stain the sauce. Cover and remove from heat.

PASTA

- Boil bow tie pasta in salted water until al dente. Strain.

SHKIAFFING IT TOGETHER

- In a big bowl mix 4 cups of pasta with a ladleful of gorgonzola sauce. Place about 1 cup of pasta on each plate. Add 2 to 3 tablespoons sauce and lots of Portobello chunks. Serve with a full-bodied amber wine.

Grocery List

- Unsalted butter (1 tablespoon)
- Portobello mushrooms (3, cut into bite-sized chunks)
- Garlic (1 clove, degermed and crushed)
- S&P
- Half & half 15% MF (2 cups)
- Crumbled Gorgonzola cheese (⅓ cup)
- Bow tie pasta (1 package, 450g)
- Full-bodied amber wine (pompous recommendation: Oslavje 2002)

Gear

- Medium frying pan
- Large saucepan
- Large pot

RADIKON OSLAVJE 2002

Amber wine is rare . . . Did you know that my eyes glow amber in the moonlight? Yea, that's right. Oslavje 2002 is just as intense. This baby is a white wine that's processed like a red, and you drink it like a red—at room temperature. It's full-bodied, robust, but has the whimsical aroma of honey and ripe yellow fruit. Which ripe yellow fruit? That's none of your business, just remember that the finish is long, hard, and spicy. AMBER POWER 4 LIFE!

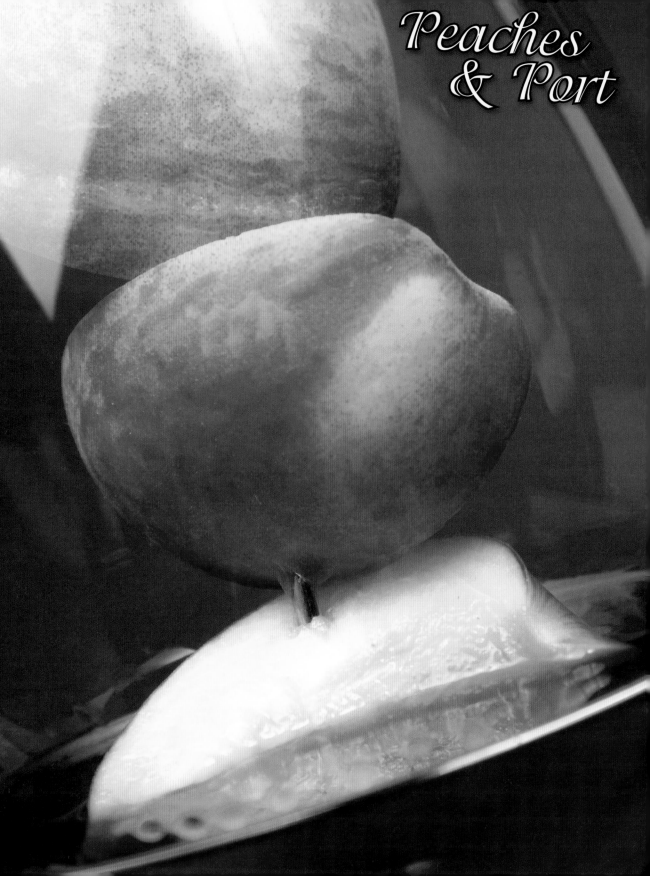

Peaches
& Port

Round 3: TKO

After a big meal like this one, your in-laws will appreciate a light, fruity dessert. (And you'll appreciate how the port wine will have them calling a cab in no time.)

Servings: 4

SHKIAFFING IT TOGETHER

- Pit peaches and slice into quarters. Impale the quarters from one peach onto a skewer, repeat for 3 more portions.
- Pour 1 to 2 ounces of aged port into each wine glass and drop a peach skewer in each.
- Serve with a square of dark chocolate on the side.

Grocery List

- Ripe peaches (4)
- Aged Port wine (pompous recommendation: Domaine Des Schistes Maury 2004)
- Dark chocolate, 65% cacao (1 bar of your favorite)

Gear

- Skewers (4)
- Large wine glasses (4)

CHAPTER.7

BREAK UP BONANZA

This meal is dedicated to the Last Supper, and it ain't the King James version. I'm talking about the last meal you'll ever make for that not-so-special someone, the meal that says, "It's over Stinkypants, your band sucked anyway!"

You're probably asking yourself: "Why stuff 'em and chuck 'em?" Well, you don't want to dump them in public, because that's mean—sorry, I misplaced the s—because that *means* being seen in public with the twit. Secondly, you want to leave them with a good taste in their mouth. Remember: You once cared for them, but more importantly, they know your secrets and probably got them on tape. As my grandmother used to say, "Revenge is a dish best served on YouTube." So, be nice.

Now granted, if the dumpee is a two-timing tequila shag, then don't bother making a meal. A five-word e-mail with a picture of food is sufficient. But if you've spent some quality time with this person (or they owe you money), then these meals will soften the blow, and/or allow you to collect.

Now I know that breaking up is never easy . . . that's why most people get married! But be strong and know that there's more to a relationship than a warm body to watch *The Wire* with! You only live once, so give the world a bra wedgie, a really hard one, then climb the fire escape and scream, just flail your arms and keep screaming. OK. Let's shkoff.

SPLITSVILLE SALAD
WITH CARAMELIZED FIGS

Basil is a sad and beautiful herb. It reminds me of my first wife Sophia.... What I remember most was her love for cooking and orgies. When we were together she would dream of becoming a dancer, like a ballerina or a stripper. Eventually we had to go our separate ways: I went to Los Angeles and she went to hell. But still, I miss Sophia! Maybe one day we'll meet again at a romantic resort like Hedonism in Jamaica.

Salad is the perfect starter for a break-up meal because it's light. Heavy dishes make us lethargic. "One more night" turns into a week, a week into a year, and before you know it, you've got three beta rugrats screeching for their Ritalin Rigatoni, and you've lost control of your life and the remote—not good.

Servings: 2

CARAMELIZED FIGS

- Cut figs into ¼-inch slices; place in an even layer on large baking dish. Drizzle figs with olive oil and broil 10 minutes.

SHKIAFFING IT TOGETHER

- In a big bowl, mix Mesclun lettuce with a teaspoon of pesto.
- Place the salad in Asian take-out cartons, which whisper: "I'm playful . . . now get the fuck out."
- Top with caramelized figs and a dollop of goat cheese. Drizzle with aged balsamic.

Grocery List

- Ripe figs (3)
- Extra virgin olive oil (1 tablespoon)
- Mesclun lettuce (small bag)
- Pesto, recipe on page 77 (1 teaspoon)
- Goat cheese (¼ cup)
- Aged balsamic vinegar, minimum 7 years old
- S&P

Gear

- Large baking dish
- Big mixing bowl
- Asian take-out cartons

nadvice

Get creative! I like to serve this salad with a fortune cookie that brings a message of hope, like "Someday you'll find someone who's actually attracted to you."

REVERSE BLT

Sandwiches are ideal for a break-up main course because they're quick and easy. Let's face it: Your soon-to-be ex was more filler than a hot dog at the homeless shelter, so save your energy for the celebratory stripper later on!

Servings: 2

THE "TOAST"

- Beat the eggs in a bowl. Cut the tomatoes into ½-inch slices, select the largest rounds, dip them in the eggs, and coat with Italian-seasoned bread crumbs.
- Heat ¼ inch of olive oil in a large frying pan. Throw in some tester bread crumbs, when crumbs start sizzling wildly (in about 10 minutes) flash fry the breaded tomatoes until golden brown all over, about 15 to 30 seconds per side. Place tomatoes on paper towels to sop up any excess oil.

THE BACON

- Well, fry up bacon until crisp.

SHKIAFFING IT TOGETHER

- Grab a fried tomato slice, top it with some bacon, add lots of Butterhead lettuce, slap on some mayo, and top off the sandwich with a second fried tomato slice.

Grocery List
- Eggs (2)
- Large, firm tomatoes (2)
- Italian-seasoned bread crumbs
- Extra virgin olive oil
- Canadian bacon (8 strips)
- Butterhead lettuce
- Mayonnaise

Gear
- Small bowl
- Large frying pan

> I once did 876 push-ups on my fists.

God's TEMPLE

MASCARPONE ♥ HONEY TOAST

This dessert is so simple, yet so delicious. If you can slice bread, you can make this dessert, literally. But if this spoonful of honey doesn't help the medicine go down, then you can always pull out the big guns and tell them that you're gay, straight, or born again. Tsaketa! That one always works.

Servings: 2

SHKIAFFING IT TOGETHER

- Slice a loaf of hazelnut bread diagonally and toast.
- Slather on some rich mascarpone cheese.
- Drizzle with wild honey.

Grocery List
- Hazelnut bread
- Mascarpone cheese
- Wild honey

Gear
- Toaster

CHAPTER.8

Make-up Soups

everybody makes mistakes. So maybe porn wasn't the best Valentine's Day present. Or maybe flying into a drunken rage isn't considered a cool party trick anymore. *Pfft.* That's okay! Because nothing says "Sorry for the syphilis" like a hot, rich bowl of homemade soup!

This chapter is devoted to soup because it's the best way to say you're sorry. Anyone can buy flowers! But within a soup you've got effort, love . . . and depending on what you did wrong, maybe even a little bit of Valium.

Make sure you take the time to make the stocks from scratch. Hey, your victim deserves a little extra love. Plus, you always need stock for other recipes, so it's win-win. As the old Italian saying goes: "Prosciutto is best kept in the cold room, otherwise it gets too warm." Think about it.

THE WORST THING I'VE EVER DONE
Come up with that stupid "Nadmit" title.

THE 2ND WORST THING I'VE EVER DONE: I once got sick of a boyfriend (he had this annoying habit of breathing.) Anyways, I decided that it would be easier to cheat on him than to break up. But since we worked together and shared a central e-mail in-box, I needed a more low-profile way to communicate with hot prospects. So I created a secret Hotmail account. One day he used my computer to innocently check his Hotmail and the login box read:
Username: NadiaGfromTheClub@hotmail.com
Man, did I ever learn a big lesson that day...
always clear your cache.

Make-up Minestrone

Minestrone is an Italian vegetable soup, so feel free to add whatever vegetables you like. In my version we'll highlight the crisp flavor of deep-seeded regret . . . now that's good stuff!

Servings: 4–6

- Heat olive oil in a soup pot on medium.
- Finely chop the onion (remember to stand real close to the onion, it'll give you that teary-eyed look) and throw it in the pot. Add in the carrots, celery, potato cubes, a small pinch of sea salt, and freshly cracked pepper to taste. Sauté 10 minutes.
- Pour in the homemade chicken stock, add cherry tomatoes, and a big pinch of Greek oregano. Simmer 20 minutes.
- Add zucchinis and cannellini beans. Simmer another 15 minutes.

SHKIAFFING IT TOGETHER

- Take the soup off the heat, and I'll show you how to get your ass off the burner through sweet presentation. Use a big bowl, because the more they eat, the less they complain. Add a dollop of pesto in the center, sprinkle with Parmesan cheese, and serve with crusty Italian bread. Try and make the ambience gentle and relaxing: tea lights, soft music, a happy ending.

Grocery List

- Extra virgin olive oil (2 tablespoons)
- Large onion (1)
- Carrots (2, thinly sliced)
- Celery (2 ribs, thinly sliced)
- Large potato (1, cut into ½-inch cubes)
- S&P
- Homemade chicken stock, see recipe on page 39 (6 cups)
- Sweet cherry tomatoes (10, cut in half)
- Dried Greek oregano
- Zucchinis (2, thinly sliced)
- Cannellini beans (450g can)
- Pesto, see recipe on page 77. (½ teaspoon)
- Parmigiano Reggiano
- Crusty Italian bread

Gear

- Soup pot

5 TRICKS TO LOOK REMORSEFUL

1. As they vent, squint your eyes and nod your head a lot. This makes you look like you're really listening and not thinking about those over-priced cherry red heels you want.

2. At intervals sigh deeply, tighten your lips and then gaze off to the side. Stare top-left and it looks like you're asking God to save your wretched soul. Stare bottom-left, and tsaketa!, you've got instant shame. Alternate. If you shake your head while you do this, you'll get even more points.

3. Don't try to explain yourself, just say "I know." The less you talk, the less you incriminate yourself. Just agree with whatever they say.

4. Buy them something expensive. Money may not buy love, but it can buy forgiveness. If you're broke, you can always make them something by hand, and then add "cheap-ass" to your list of things to apologize for.

5. Swear on your life that you'll never do it again (until next time).

This is one of my favorite soups. One whiff of this and you'll have your loved one saying, "Affair? *Schmaffair* . . . now pass the cheddar!"

Servings: 4–6

PREP

- Soak the chipotle pepper in water for a few hours to reconstitute.
- Seed and chop the pepper.

SOUP BASE

- In a soup pot, heat olive oil on medium heat. Then add chopped onion and chopped chipotle pepper. Sauté for 5 minutes.
- Turn the heat to medium-low and add homemade chicken stock, roasted cherry tomatoes, a sprig of fresh epazote, cumin, and sea salt, and freshly cracked pepper to taste. Stir and simmer for 30 minutes, then discard epazote sprig.

SHKIAFFING IT TOGETHER

- Ladle the soup into serving bowls. Add ripe avocado slices and sprinkle with fine aged cheddar. Then top with a mound of crispy tortilla strips.

Grocery List

- Dried chipotle pepper (1)
- Extra virgin olive oil (1 tablespoon)
- Small white onion (1, chopped)
- Homemade chicken stock, see recipe on page 39 (6 cups)
- Roasted cherry tomatoes, see recipe on page 167.
- Fresh epazote (1 sprig)
- Cumin
- S&P
- Avocado (1)
- Aged cheddar, minimum 5 years old
- Fried tortilla strips

Gear

- Soup pot
- Shallow baking dish

The epazote plant is also known as Mexican tea and the flavor is difficult to describe. When it is fresh it reminds me of the Sambuca taste of anise, mint, and medicine. When it is dried it tastes like rotting old bark. Try and get it fresh, use little, and never go to Brazil in July... It is cold!

Contrite Clam Chowder

Who can stay angry at someone who makes them a bowl of creamy homemade clam chowder? The lactose-intolerant, maybe. But those people are like vegans, they don't count.

Servings: 4–6

- Heat a soup pot over medium heat. Add bacon strips and fry until crisp. Place bacon on paper towels to absorb excess oil and set aside. Keep the bacon grease in the pot.
- To the bacon grease add diced yellow onion and sauté until soft, about 8 minutes. Add potato cubes and clam juice. Reduce heat to low and simmer 15 minutes, until potatoes are tender.
- Stir in whole milk and heavy cream. The minute it looks like it's going to boil, turn the heat down to low.
- Then add clam meat and pinches of sea salt and freshly cracked pepper. Stir and let clam meat warm through, about 5 to 8 minutes.

SHKIAFFING IT TOGETHER

- Ladle soup into bowls. Sprinkle with a handful of minced fresh parsley and crumble the bacon on top. Serve with thick slices of crusty bread.

Grocery List
- Canadian bacon (8 strips)
- Yellow onion (2, diced)
- Yukon Gold potato (2, chopped into ½-inch cubes)
- All-natural clam juice (1 cup)
- Whole milk, 3.25% MF (2 cups)
- Heavy Cream, 35% MF (2 cups)
- All-natural baby clam meat (2 cups)
- S&P
- Fresh parsley (1 bunch)
- Crusty bread

Gear
- Soup pot

Bro, back when I was a kid my favorite Greek superhero **"έξοχος χταπόδι άνδρας"** taught me dat der's nutting you can't fix with clams. But den I got older, bro. I realized dat no matter how many clams are involved, der's certain tings dat can never be forgiven. You can forget, but never forgive.

Next time, just don't get caught!

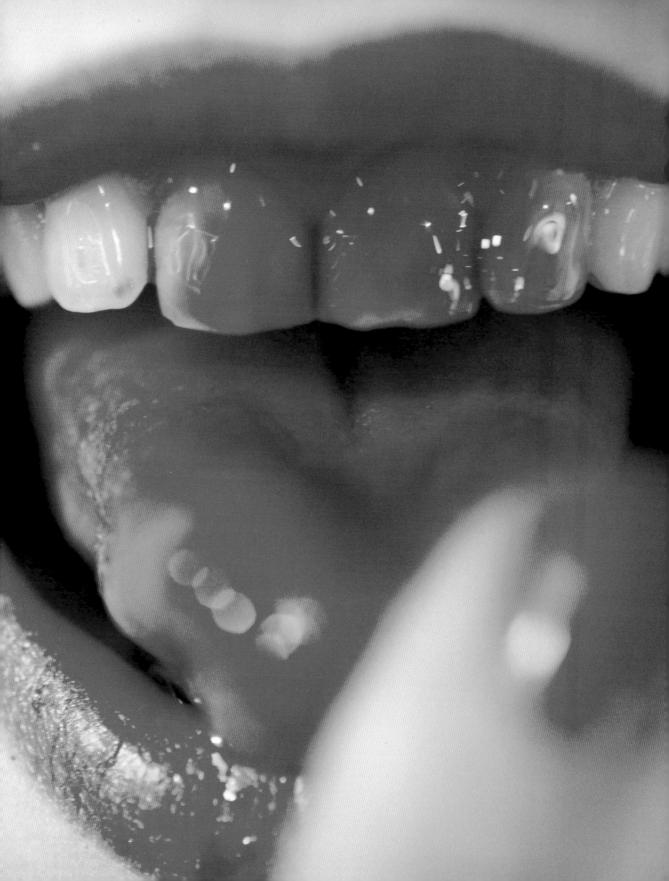

CHAPTER.9

HALLOWEEN HOOTENANNY

*S*ome people just don't get Halloween. "I'm too mature to dress up! I'm too mature to throw eggs at the homeless!" WHATEVER! These people have no spirit.

I don't care what anyone says, Halloween is scary. Computer nerds puffed up in pimp costumes, sloppy chicks in cheap bunny suits, and that I-couldn't-think-of-a-costume confused guy in pajamas and smeared lipstick. And the horror doesn't stop there, oh no! Halloween means winter's coming, so the desperate need for a warm body may just have you hooking up with pajama boy . . . now that's truly terrifying.

Every year I throw a kick-ass Halloween party, and this year you're invited . . . to read about how I prepare it.

The first thing you need when you're throwing a Halloween party is a good costume, and rentals are definitely the way to go. Buying a one-off is simply a waste of cash . . . unless you have ulterior motives for a latex nun's suit. The second thing you want to do is decorate, and it doesn't take much to turn your home into a nightmarish crypt: a couple of black candles, some bloodstained sheets, a screeching soundtrack of Rachael Ray's laughter . . . and finally, you need some scary treats!

MWAHAHAHAHA!

BOCCONCINI EYEBALLS

Nothing says Halloween like these suckers. They don't sacrifice taste for terror, plus you'll get a good laugh from your guests

Servings: 8

BOCCONCINI EYEBALLS

- Slice green olives into ¼-inch disks. Place an olive disk in the center of a bocconcino and trace around it with a sharp paring knife. Carve out a ½-inch chunk of cheese from the outline and pop in the olive disk.
- Wrap a slice of fleshy prosciutto around the bocconcini eyeball. Look proudly upon your creation and repeat with the rest of the bocconcini.

ITALIAN BLOOD SALSA

- Pour whole can of San Marzano tomatoes into a bowl, then add olive oil, aged balsamic vinegar, garlic, red onion, parsley, basil, a big pinch of dried Greek oregano, a small pinch of hot chile flakes, 2 big pinches of salt, 3 big pinches of sugar, and lots of freshly cracked pepper.
- Squish all ingredients together with your bare hands to mix; set aside.

SHKIAFFING IT TOGETHER

- Divide eyeballs into pairs, slap onto individual plates, and add a couple of tablespoons of salsa to each. Serve with crostini.

Grocery List
- Large green olives stuffed with pimento (8)
- Bocconcini cheese balls (16)
- Prosciutto di Parma (nitrate free) (8 slices)
- Whole San Marzano tomatoes (796 ml can)
- Extra virgin olive oil (3 tablespoons)
- Aged balsamic vinegar (1 teaspoon)
- Garlic (2 cloves, degermed and minced)
- Red onion (1, minced)
- Fresh flat-leaf parsley (handful, finely chopped)
- Fresh basil (handful, finely chopped)
- Dried Greek oregano
- Hot chile flakes
- Brown sugar
- S&P
- Crostini

Gear
- Paring knife
- Medium-sized mixing bowl

Halloween is ridiculous. If you ask me, playing dress-up is for little girls, not for hardened men! Pfft. All that dancing around, dressed in cheap costumes, with heavy chains around your neck, while three hairy women tie you up and shout: "Who's the bitch now? Who's the bitch now, Yeheskel?!" And you can't even call the police, because you paid the women to come over, and you put the chains around your own neck!

So they keep slapping you, as you kneel there sweating, chafing, frantically applying more lipstick . . . always more lipstick . . . BUT THEY ARE NEVER SATISFIED!!!

Umm, Hey! Anybody like oregano? Because the best oregano comes from Greece. Ding-ding. Oops, did you hear that? I think my toast is ready, I must go now.

CREEP-A-LICIOUS
COFFIN SANDWICHES

This sandwich is so pretty . . . um, I mean petrifying.

Servings: 8

PESTO

- Into a food processor throw fresh basil, grated parmesan, garlic, and toasted pine nuts. (To toast nuts: Heat them in a dry pan on medium-high for 8 to 10 minutes, stirring often. When they begin to turn a golden brown take them out of the pan.) While processing, add olive oil in a steady stream until smooth. Set aside.

SANDWICHES

- Cut the pumpernickel bread into ½-inch slices, then into coffin shapes.
- On each slice of bread, stack a layer of mayo, a layer of pesto, a sprinkling of toasted almonds, some Alfalfa sprouts, a layer of sliced McIntosh apples, and some crumbled cheddar.
- Place another coffin-shaped bread slice on top and repeat for another layer. Top off with a final coffin slice.

Grocery List
- Fresh basil (2 packed cups)
- Parmigiano Reggiano (½ cup, grated)
- Garlic (1 clove, degermed)
- Pine nuts (¼ cup)
- Extra virgin olive oil (½ cup)
- Pumpernickel bread (1 large loaf)
- Mayonnaise
- Almond slivers (1 cup)
- Alfalfa sprouts (2 cups)
- McIntosh apples (8, sliced)
- Aged cheddar, minimum 5 years old (2 cups)

Gear
- Food processor
- Medium-sized frying pan

nadvice

You can also replace the cheddar with creamy brie cheese, and the apples with crisp cucumbers. Enjoy this sandwich anytime—minus the coffin-shaped bread. Unless you're a Goth . . . then you can just get a life.

SEVERED-HAND
SANGRIA

I'm not a fan of sweet drinks, so this recipe for sangria is quite dry. Give it a shot. If you prefer it sweeter, you know what to do . . . stay away from the girly drinks and grow some freakin' hair on your chest.

Servings: 10 glasses

SHKIAFFING IT TOGETHER

- The night before the party, fill a few latex gloves with some filtered water, tie them up like you would a balloon and freeze overnight.
- In a big punch bowl combine red wine, sparkling water, orange juice, brandy, brown sugar, fruit slices, and sour cherry syrup.
- Stir and add one frozen ice-hand, latex glove removed.

Grocery List
- Latex gloves
- Filtered water
- Dry red wine (2 bottles)
- Sparkling water (3 cups)
- Freshly squeezed orange juice (3 cups)
- Brandy or Cointreau (3 ounces)
- Brown sugar (3 heaping teaspoons)
- Fresh oranges (2, thinly sliced)
- Fresh pink grapefruit (2, thinly sliced)
- Fresh lemons (2, thinly sliced)
- Fresh limes (2, thinly sliced)
- Natural sour cherries in syrup (350g jar)

Gear
- Big punch bowl

Bro, people get all nervous about finding da perfect costume. *Me I say: Relax. Slap an octopus on your head and relax bro, because dat shit is scary.

CHAPTER. 10

PMSCAPADES

When I'm PMS-ing I *crave* the combination of sweet and salty. Now I'm not talking about a measly peanut butter cup or two, I'm talking *hardcore*: chips smothered in Swedish chocolate fondue, hot banana curries, fleur de sel caramel drizzled onto fine French cheeses . . . you get the idea. This chapter is for the very adventurous, or the very bloated.

Besides getting a little crazy in the sweet/savory department, I also get a wee bit sentimental. Music will make me cry, and not particularly sappy tunes either. If you're ever driving around the LA area and hear someone sobbing loudly in her car to The Cramps, it's me, and it's mid-month. Believe it or not I also get aggressive. I've been kicked out of many a bar—Oh wait, that's just because I'm an asshole when I'm drunk.

Anyhoo . . . when you're hormonally taxed, give yourself a break. Eat what you want, abuse whomever you please. They'll forgive you . . . hey, you're PMS-ing! Just flash them your badge and remember to carry it with pride (and rage and sadness and exaggerated empathy and jogging pants)!

BITCHIN' PMS CLUB

Interacting with the proprietor of this badge is at your own risk. Proprietor is in no way responsible for any violent acts, emotional or otherwise, that may occur during the seven-to-fourteen day period during which this badge is carried. If you have any complaints about the proprietor's behavior during this time, please refrain from addressing her directly and forward your grievances to: pmsabuse@bitchinkitchen.tv.

> I'm staying outta this one, bro.

CHOCOLATE FONDUE

Why the sweet and salty cravings? The hormonal riptides of PMS squash the production of "happy chemical" serotonin in your brain. One way you can produce serotonin is by eating carbs, and that's where these cravings come from. But some doctors claim that "you don't have to eat chocolate or potato chips to do that any more than you need to drink champagne to satisfy your thirst."

Pfft. They know nothing of my thirst.

They also recommend trying healthy snacks such as "tuna on a piece of rye crisp." Hehe. Try offering a tuna crisp to your girlfriend when she's PMSing and see what happens . . . no really, try it.

Servings: 1 massive, dirty shkoff-fest

FONDUE

- Place a double boiler over medium-low heat and combine Toblerone, dark chocolate, and whipping cream. Stir until melted.
- Rip open the bags of chips and pretzels and dip them in the creamy fondue. Make sure you get lots of chocolatey crumbs all over your face and pajamas; this way you can really feel sorry for yourself afterward.

Grocery List

- Toblerone, or any high-end Swedish honey-nougat milk chocolate (2 cups, roughly chopped)
- Dark bittersweet chocolate (½ cup)
- Whipping cream, 35% MF (½ cup)
- Muncho chips (1 big bag)
- Pretzels (1 big bag)

Gear

- Double boiler (or a pot and a large, thick plastic mixing bowl)

CHICKEN & BANANA CURRY

nadvice

Relax, baby! When you're PMSing remember that you look worse than you feel!

Crunchy almonds, tender chicken pieces, tart raisins, smothered in a . . . Bah, who am I: Giada De Laurentiis?! Fuck it. This curry rocks hard.

Servings: 4
- Marinate the chicken breasts for 24 hours.

CURRY SPICE
- Heat a small, dry pan over medium heat. Then add hot curry powder. Stir often, until fragrant, about 30 seconds. Set aside.

TOASTED ALMONDS
- Add slivered almonds to another dry pan over medium-high heat. Keep stirring until the nuts become golden in color, about 7 to 10 minutes. (Always watch nuts carefully when you're toasting them, because they go from tasty to burnt in a split-second.)
- Once they toast, remove nuts from the pan (or they'll keep toasting and burn.) Set aside.

CHICKEN
- Heat olive oil in a large frying pan over medium heat. Add garlic cloves and sauté for 2 minutes until golden.
- Throw in the finely chopped onions and sauté for 8 minutes more. Remove onions and garlic and set aside, reserving the oil.
- Wipe down the marinated chicken and cut into bite-size pieces. Pour some flour on a plate. Add a big pinch of salt and freshly cracked pepper. Mix. Toss chicken pieces in flour to lightly coat.
- Fry chicken on medium heat in the same pan/oil as you cooked the onions, until golden brown on all sides, about 10 minutes. Set aside.

CURRY SAUCE
- Heat a large saucepan over medium heat. Add water, the toasted curry spice, brown sugar, turmeric, the juice of 1 large lemon, hot mango chutney, raisins, and the toasted almond slivers. Stir and bring to a simmer.

THICKENER
- In a measuring cup combine homemade chicken stock and 2 tablespoons flour.
- Mix well.
- Pass liquid through a sieve to remove any flour chunks. Add to the curry sauce and mix well.
- Turn the heat down to medium-low and to the curry sauce add the sautéed onions and garlic, the crisped chicken, and sea salt and freshly cracked pepper to taste. Cook for 30 minutes.

SHKIAFFING IT TOGETHER
- Ladle some chicken curry on a plate and shkoff with sliced ripe bananas, sweet shredded coconut, hot mango chutney, and raisins.

Grocery List
- Chicken breasts (2)
- Chicken marinade, see recipe on page 115
- Hot curry powder (2 tablespoons)
- Slivered almonds (½ cup)
- Extra virgin olive oil (2 tablespoons)
- Garlic (2 cloves, degermed and crushed)
- Large onions (2, finely chopped)
- Flour
- S&P
- Water (1½ cups)
- Brown sugar (2 tablespoons)
- Turmeric (1 teaspoon)
- Large lemon (1)
- Hot mango chutney (3 tablespoons)
- Dark raisins (½ cup)
- Homemade chicken stock, see recipe on page 39 (1 cup)
- Ripe bananas (2, sliced)
- Sweet shredded coconut

Gear
- 2 small frying pans
- Large frying pan
- Large saucepan
- Measuring cup
- Sieve

CURRY-TASTIC

Here's a recipe for an awesome curry sauce that goes with almost anything . . . that goes with curry sauce.

Servings: 2–3

CURRY

- Heat olive oil in a large saucepan over medium heat and sauté garlic for 2 minutes until golden.
- Add diced red onion and sauté for about 8 minutes.
- Add tomatoes, stir and simmer 10 minutes.
- Add chicken stock, diced potatoes, lentils, toasted curry powder, brown sugar, and a big pinch of cayenne pepper. Turn heat down to medium-low and simmer 30 minutes.
- Taste the curry and add sea salt, freshly cracked pepper, and/or sugar as needed.
- Rinse baby spinach and pat dry. Throw it in the sauce, stir until wilted.
- Stir in 1 to 2 tablespoons plain yogurt, if desired.
- Shkoff with buttered naan bread or rice.

Grocery List

- Extra virgin olive oil (2 tablespoons)
- Garlic (2 cloves, degermed and crushed)
- Small red onion (1, diced)
- Large ripe tomatoes (4, roughly chopped)
- Homemade chicken stock, see recipe on page 39 (2 cups)
- Large potatoes (2, diced into ½-inch cubes)
- Lentils (1 can)
- Hot curry powder (1 tablespoon)
- Brown sugar (1 tablespoon)
- Cayenne pepper
- S&P
- Sugar
- Fresh baby spinach (2 cups)
- Plain yogurt (optional)
- naan or wild rice

Gear

- 1 large saucepan

The best advice I ever got from my father was this:
1. "When your woman is PMS-ing, do not take anything she says seriously—just pretend you do."
2. "Always spit in the toilet before you pee so you can aim better." Now that this is clear, let us talk about curry.
   Contrary to popular belief, curry powder does not come from bonsai trees ripe with baby curry berries. No! Curry is a mix of many spices: coriander, fenugreek, turmeric, and cumin are the most popular. Depending on the recipe, additional ingredients like ginger, fennel seed, garlic, clove, cinnamon, long pepper, mustard seed, black cardamom, green cardamom, mace, nutmeg, red pepper, black pepper, and snake testicles are used in varying quantities.

GRANNY SMITH
BRIE & CARAMEL

Making homemade caramel can be a bit dangerous, but who doesn't enjoy a little second-degree burn every now and then?

Servings: 2

CARAMEL

- Heat a large pan over medium-low heat. Add filtered water and castor sugar. Cook until sugar completely dissolves and begins to caramelize.
- When sugar is a deep golden color, add butter, whipping cream, and a big pinch of fleur de sel—Be careful! When adding the butter and cream, it'll sputter and hiss. Try not to get burned. Mwahahaha! Oops, did I just cackle *in writing*? I'm sorry, I meant: Whisk vigorously until smooth.
- Take off heat and let caramel cool. (It will last a good week in the fridge.)

PLATING

- Slice Granny Smith apples in half, removing core. Place in one or two bowls. Add a big chunk of your favorite Brie cheese (Camembert is great, too). Drizzle with lots of creamy caramel.

Grocery List

- Filtered water (½ cup)
- Ultra-fine castor sugar[2], or pulverize granulated sugar in the food processor for a few seconds (1 cup)
- Unsalted butter (¼ cup)
- Whipping cream, 35%MF (1 cup)
- Fleur de sel
- Granny Smith apples (2)
- Brie cheese

Gear

- Large stainless steel pan (you need to be able to see the color of the sugar change)
- Whisk
- Guts

[2]I know I told you white sugar is bad, and it is . . . but this is *caramel* baby, you gotta make an exception.

nadvice

Some of you may read this recipe for caramel, see that it calls for pulverized sugar, and say to yourselves: "Hmm, I think I have some confectioners' sugar collecting dust in the back of the cupboard from that brownie experiment back in 1996. That stuff looks pulverized to me . . ." Stop right there, Bucko. Confectioners' sugar has starch in it, which will ruin your caramel. And let's be honest here: When are you ever going to use that confectioners' sugar? Just throw it away man, throw it away.

BACK TA

sex-Life savers:
a chapter for the Boys

German study shows that women's sex drives take a dive in long-term relationships, but as they say, you don't need a weatherman to know which way the wind *doesn't* blow.

Why do women lose interest? Well this study proposes that chicks become frigid because of the laws of supply and demand, subconsciously keeping their "resources" scarce to hold buddy's interest. Compelling theory, but it seems like years of public farting and sports highlights as foreplay may be the real answer.

Guys, if she'd rather watch "Dancing with the B-List" than tango with you, it's time to do something romantic. You may think oysters and bubbly are the ticket to getting some action, but an elaborate spread makes it clear that she's dessert—and there's nothing worse than pressure to kill a mood that's already on life support. That's why this chapter is devoted to recipes that are subtle and comforting. As an added bonus, they're also super easy to make, because the last thing you need is something complicated . . . like replacing toilet paper rolls, or listening. Tsk-tsk.

nadvice

Relax, every relationship hits a bedroom low at one time or another. Actually, let me rephrase that: Boys, stop picking your nose in front of your girlfriend and maybe you'll get some action.

SHEPHERD'S PIE

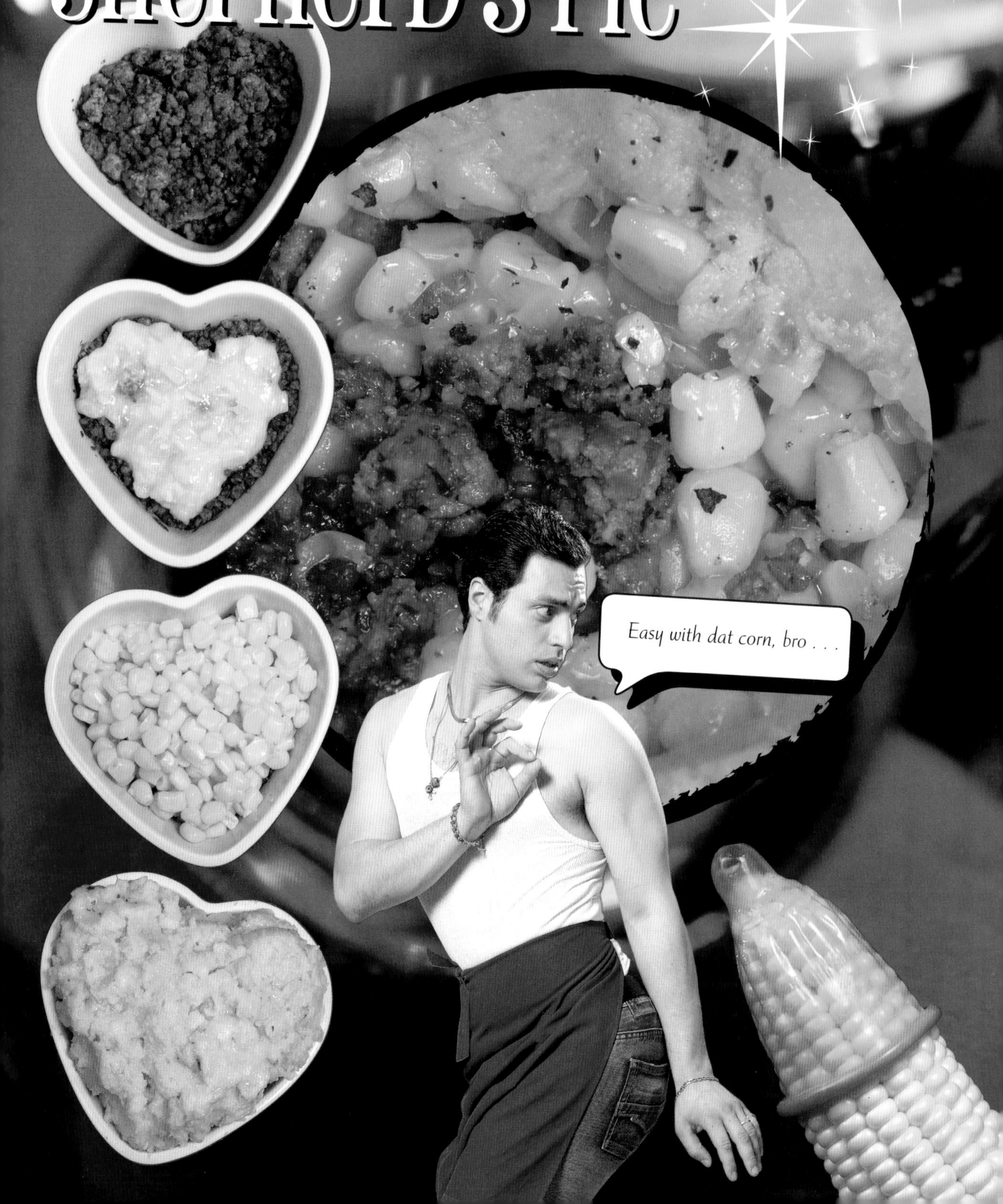

This Shepherd's Pie will last and satisfy for days . . . hey, something's got to.

Servings: 4 (plus a delicious breakfast-in-bed for two)

BEEF

- Heat olive oil in a sauté pan over medium heat. Add minced garlic and sauté for 2 minutes until golden.
- Add minced red onion and sauté 5 minutes.
- Add lean ground beef, a small pinch of sea salt, and freshly cracked pepper to taste.
- Cook, stirring for about 10 minutes.
- Turn the heat up to medium-high and crisp the meat for another 3 to 5 minutes. Add minced parsley and take it off the heat.

POTATOES

- Chop sweet potato and russet potatoes in equal-sized chunks for even cooking.
- Bring a pot of salted water to a boil. Drop the potato slices into the water and cook until fork-tender, about 15 minutes. Strain.
- Put the strained potatoes in a big bowl, add butter, milk, a big pinch of salt, and freshly cracked pepper to taste. Smash roughly, don't puree.

SHKIAFFING IT TOGETHER

Presentation is as key to this Shepherd's Pie as it is to your relationship. If you think back to when she couldn't wait to get you home, chances are you weren't strutting around in ratty briefs, scratching and sniffing to your heart's content. So put some pants on and let's plate this proper.

Heart-shaped ramekins are a lifesaver. They fake emotion better than a stripper at last call. Want a woman to feel special, but the game's on? Slap some chips in a heart-shaped ramekin, and, poof! *Special Chips!* Want to reap the benefits of breakfast in bed but you're too lazy to fry an egg? Slap some Cheerios in a heart-shaped ramekin and, poof! *Special Cheerios!* I'm telling you, the energy you save by letting the ramekin do the talking is worth its weight in gold. With all that said . . .

- Spoon a thick layer of crisped beef into the bottom of four heart-shaped ramekins, then add a thin layer of creamed corn, a thin layer of sweet corn niblets, and a thick layer of smashed potatoes. Sprinkle with Panko crumbs.
- Broil in the oven 10 to 15 minutes, until the top is golden brown.

Grocery List
- *Extra virgin olive oil (2 tablespoons)*
- *Garlic (1 clove, degermed and minced)*
- *Large red onion (1, minced)*
- *Lean ground beef (1 pound)*
- *S&P*
- *Fresh parsley (handful)*
- *Sweet potato (1)*
- *Russet potatoes (2)*
- *Unsalted butter (1 tablespoon)*
- *Whole milk, 3.25% MF (3 tablespoons)*
- *Creamed corn (450g can)*
- *Sweet corn niblets (450g can)*
- *Panko crumbs*

Gear
- *Sauté pan*
- *Large pot*
- *Large mixing bowl*

People say that lean beef is too dry; I completely disagree. It's all about how you prepare it. Just like a relationship, juiciness comes with the little things: adding spice, massaging it with a little oil . . . letting it warm up slowly instead of thrusting it onto an overheated pan for 15 minutes and expecting a succulent cut that's ready to go!

BLUE-CHEESE BURGERS
with caramelized onions & truffle aioli

In the Bitchin' Basics I mentioned how important it is to buy organic foods, especially when it comes to meat. If you haven't been taking my advice, now's the time to start. Since this burger is served medium-rare—and is so juicy that it'll be dripping down your chin—you need to *only use fresh organic chuck*. No excuses or exceptions. If you follow this recipe using cheap ground beef, well . . . let's just say that you definitely won't be getting laid in the hospital.

Servings: 4

TRUFFLE AIOLI

- Pour olive oil into a measuring cup with a lip. Add truffle oil, mix, and set aside.
- In a food processor add garlic, a pinch of sea salt, Dijon mustard, and egg yolks.
- Blend until smooth. Keep blending and slowly pour in ½ cup of the olive-truffle oil mixture in a thin stream. Do this very slowly, otherwise it won't emulsify/thicken.
- Still blending, add lemon juice and water. Then slowly add the rest of the oil in a thin stream. The mixture will thicken as you continue to blend it. When it's slightly thinner than store-bought mayo, it's done. You can add more lemon juice and S&P to taste.

MEAT

- Set the grill on high heat. Separate the meat into four pieces. Loosely shape meat into 1-inch thick patties, don't over-handle.
- Sprinkle the patties with a small pinch of salt and freshly cracked pepper. Sear patties for 2 minutes on each side. Turn the grill down to medium heat and cook patties for another 3 minutes per side (for medium rare burgers). Take the patties off the heat and let them rest for 5 minutes.

SHKIAFFING IT TOGETHER

- Toast the onion buns, slather them with 1 heaping tablespoon of truffle aioli and add grilled burger patties. Top with 1 heaping tablespoon of Danish blue cheese, tons of sweet caramelized onions, and serve with a glass of dry red wine.

Grocery List
- Extra virgin olive oil (1 cup)
- Truffle oil (1 tablespoon)
- Garlic (4 cloves, degermed)
- S&P
- Dijon mustard (1 teaspoon)
- Eggs (2)
- Fresh lemon juice (1 tablespoon)
- Water (½ teaspoon)
- Fresh organic ground chuck (1 pound)
- Artisanal onion buns (4)
- Danish blue cheese (⅓ cup)
- Caramelized onions, see recipe on page 25.

Gear
- Measuring cup with a lip
- Food processor
- Grill

nadvice

If this doesn't get you some action, you can always find a hobby to distract you from your crappy sex life, like golf . . . or reproducing.

Penne with Broccoli Rabe & Spicy Italian Sausage

This pasta relies on the spicy sausage oils to make a light "sauce." That's why it's important to use the best Italian sausage you can get your hands on. *That means go to a fine butcher to buy the sausages.* Remember guys, we're trying to get away from the cheap sausage party that only you can enjoy, not cook up another one.

Servings: 4

BROCCOLI RABE

- Rinse broccoli rabe. Cut off and discard 1 inch from end of stems. Bring a pot of salted water to a boil. Add the broccoli rabe and boil, uncovered, until tender (about 3 minutes). Strain.
- Place broccoli rabe in a large bowl filled with ice water for 2 minutes to stop the cooking process; strain and set aside.

ITALIAN SAUSAGE

- Remove sausage casing.
- Heat a large pan over medium heat and add 1 tablespoon olive oil. Add minced garlic and sauté until golden, about 2 minutes.
- Add sausage meat, separate into bits with a wooden spoon, and fry for 10 to 15 minutes, until the meat is cooked and has some crispiness to it.
- Add 3 to 4 tablespoons olive oil. Introduce the broccoli rabe, mix with the sausage, and sauté 5 more minutes. Remove from heat.

PASTA

- Bring salted water to a boil and add the penne rigate. Cook until al dente, then strain.
- Add the pasta to the sausage-broccoli rabe mix. Turn the heat up to medium and sauté 5 minutes, using tongs to fully coat the pasta with the spicy sausage oils and garlicky goodness.

PLATING

- Serve the pasta with Parmesan shavings, and lots of freshly cracked pepper.

Grocery List
- Broccoli rabe (1 pound)
- S&P
- Artisanal Italian spicy sausages (4)
- Extra virgin olive oil (5 tablespoons)
- Garlic (1 clove, degermed and minced)
- Penne rigate, ridged penne (500g)
- Parmigiano Reggiano

Gear
- Large pot
- Large bowl
- Large frying pan
- Tongs

CHAPTER 12

Italian Christmas Eve

Jingle bells, Rachel smells, Martha laid an egg!
Just kidding! Martha doesn't have any eggs left.

I don't focus on many Hallmark holidays in this book, but Christmas is one of the few exceptions. For Italians, Christmas is a magical time filled with everything we hold dear: food, food, and even more food. But Italians don't eat turkey for Christmas Eve, we eat seafood, and this feast is called "La Vigilia di Natale" (pronounced *la vee-jee-lee-ya dee nat-ah-lay*). It's a tradition that celebrates the humble birth of baby Jesus—kind of like diamond-studded crosses or crusades!

In this chapter I'll dish out a festive three-course meal, but any Italian will tell you that this is a mere *appetizer* on Christmas Eve. There would be at least four more courses, three desserts, two fights, and one exceptionally loud long-distance call.

Sigh . . . let's make some mussels . . .

Mussels

Servings: 4

MUSSELS

- Scrub the mussels under cold water to remove any cac (the beard, sand, and/or general nastiness from the murky depths of the ocean). Discard any open mussels. Set aside.

SAUCE

- Set a large pot over medium-high heat and add butter and minced shallots. Sauté for 2 minutes.
- To the pot add the dry white wine, the juice of 6 fresh lemons, a handful of minced parsley, a big pinch of sea salt, and lots of freshly cracked pepper. Bring mixture to a boil, and let it boil for 3 minutes.
- Throw mussels into the pot, cover, and keep boiling on high heat. Every few minutes grab the pot and shake it around so the mussels cook evenly. In 5 minutes the shells will open and they're done.

Grocery List
- *Mussels (2 pounds)*
- *Unsalted butter (½ cup)*
- *Shallots (½ cup, minced)*
- *Dry white wine (1 cup)*
- *Lemons (6)*
- *Fresh flat-leaf parsley (handful, minced)*
- *S&P*

Gear
- *1 large stock pot with lid*

GREEK CHRISTMAS TRADITIONS

Greek Christmas is intense, bro. We fast for forty days! No meat, no milk, no nutting (only ouzo on da weekends). I get weak, bro! But dat's okay, because it's for da Big Guy. I'll do anything for da Big Guy . . . except for one ting: I won't get scammed into dat Christmas tree scam, bro! One hundred fifty dollars for a tree?! *Ya, okay! Me I just slap my wife's jewelry on da houseplants, and dat's it. Nice and festive.

Seafood Spaghetti

The one thing I love about Christmas is New Year's Eve! Every year I have a tradition of making a promise I cannot keep. Last year I promised myself no more divorces! Then me, Shlomit, and Vanessa got divorced. I know what you are thinking: How can one man divorce two women at the same time? I will put it this way: If this was Facebook, it would be Very Fucking Complicated.

Us Italians know that nothing says Baby Jesus like a plate full of extravagant seafood. But if you're in the mood for something a little lighter and less holy, just omit all critters except for the clams to make a fantastic clam spaghetti. Or you can even omit everything but the bottle of wine. Amen.

Servings: 4

SAUCE

- Heat 3 tablespoons olive oil in a large saucepan over medium heat. Add a small pinch of hot chile flakes, and crushed garlic cloves. Sauté for 2 minutes until garlic is golden.
- Pour in San Marzano tomatoes. Simmer for 10 minutes.
- Add dry white wine to the sauce. Throw in baby clams. Stir and simmer for 10 more minutes.
- Throw in a handful of minced parsley, a small pinch of sea salt, a small pinch of brown sugar, and freshly cracked pepper to taste. Stir, cover, and take off the heat.

SCALLOPS

- Rinse scallops under cold water, pat dry.
- In a sauté pan, heat 1 teaspoon butter and 1 teaspoon olive oil over medium heat. Add scallops, sprinkle with a small pinch of salt and freshly cracked pepper. Sear for 1 to 2 minutes per side until golden and crispy on the outside.

SHRIMP

- Rinse, peel, and devein the shrimp. (See Panos's tips on deveining shrimp on page 41.)

CALAMARI

- Rinse calamari under cold water, pat dry. Slice into ¼-inch rounds.

PASTA

- Boil spaghetti in salted water until al dente. Strain and set aside.

SHKIAFFING IT TOGETHER

- Heat the sauce on medium, then add the shrimp and cook 2 minutes.
- Add scallops and cook another 3 minutes.
- Add calamari, which will firm up into rings almost instantly. Cook 1 minute and remove sauce from heat.
- In a big bowl combine pasta and a ladleful of sauce, mix well with tongs.

PLATING

- Make sure each plate of pasta contains a jumbo shrimp, a scallop, some calamari, and clams. Drizzle with 2 to 3 tablespoons of sauce.

Grocery List

- Extra virgin olive oil (3 tablespoons plus 1 teaspoon)
- Hot chile flakes
- Garlic (2 cloves, degermed and crushed)
- Whole San Marzano tomatoes (796ml, crushed by hand)
- Dry white wine (½ cup)
- All natural baby clam meat with juice (1 cup)
- Fresh flat-leaf parsley (handful, minced)
- S&P
- Brown sugar
- Jumbo scallops (4)
- Unsalted butter (1 teaspoon)
- Jumbo tiger shrimp (4)
- Whole calamari (2)
- Spaghetti (450g)

Gear

- Large saucepan with lid
- Sauté pan
- Large pot
- Mixing bowl
- Tongs

Panettone Bread Pudding

If you're Italian or have lots of (cheap) Italian friends, you probably get more fucking panettone during the holiday season than you could possibly eat in a year. Last Christmas was no exception, so it got me thinking: What if I organized a panettone drive for the homeless?! Then all that thinking made me hungry, so I made bread pudding.

Servings: 6

PANETTONE

- Slice the panettone into 1-inch cubes to make about 7 cups. Place the cubes in an even layer on a baking sheet to dry out for a few hours or overnight.

PUDDING MIXTURE

- In a large mixing bowl, combine milk, 4 egg yolks (save the whites), 1 to 2 tablespoons brown sugar, and the seeds of half a vanilla bean (slice one side of the bean open lengthwise and scrape out the seeds with a sharp knife)—the other half of the seeds will be used later. Whisk together.
- Dump the panettone cubes into the pudding mixture. Mix well with your hands and let soak for 5 to 10 minutes.

MERINGUE

- Position the oven rack in the center of the oven and preheat to 350°F.
- Using a food processor or electric beater, whip the 4 egg whites with a small pinch of cream of tartar until stiff peaks form (aka meringue).
- Delicately fold the meringue into the bread pudding mixture, stir just a few times—you want to see streaks of meringue.
- Butter a soufflé mold, pour in the bread pudding mixture, and bake 1 hour.

CREME ANGLAISE

- In a medium bowl, whisk together 3 egg yolks and ¼ cup brown sugar. Set aside.
- Place a small saucepan over medium heat. Add whipping cream and the seeds from the other half of the vanilla bean. Stir cream and vanilla seeds constantly. When bubbles form around the edges (about 8 minutes), remove from heat. Do not boil.
- Stir heated vanilla-cream into egg yolk mixture, 1 tablespoon at a time. (Don't rush things; you don't want to cook the eggs.) Repeat until all the cream is incorporated.
- Pour everything back into the saucepan and cook over medium-low heat, stirring constantly and being careful not to let it boil. Cook until the mixture is thick enough to coat the back of a wooden spoon, about 3 to 5 minutes.
- Pass it through a fine wire mesh sieve, then pour cream mixture into a serving container. (If you want to make this in advance, you can place plastic wrap directly on the surface, pop it in the fridge and it'll keep for up to 2 days. Reheat over low heat.)

PLATING

- In individual serving bowls, add 1 cup warm bread pudding and a handful of berries. Drizzle with lots of Crème Anglaise.

Grocery List

- Large stale panettone, plain or with candied fruits and nuts (1)
- Whole milk, 3.25% MF (2 cups)
- Eggs (7)
- Brown sugar (2 tablespoons plus ¼ cup)
- Vanilla bean (1)
- Cream of tartar
- Unsalted butter
- Whipping cream, 35% MF (1 cup)
- Strawberries (1 cup)
- Blueberries (1 cup)

Gear

- Baking sheet
- Large mixing bowl
- Food processor or electric beater
- Medium mixing bowl
- 1 large casserole or soufflé mold. Must fit 8 cups.
- Small saucepan
- Fine wire mesh sieve

WORST CHRISTMAS GIFTS EVER

1. **Clothing Shipped from the Obscure Aunt in Italy Who You Haven't Seen in Two Decades**

Wow . . . a large T-shirt and matching pantaloons emblazoned with loud knock-off Gucci symbols! Should I try it on now or beat you with it later?

2. **Cheap Hippie Jewelry**

Peace signs, yin and yangs, dolphins . . . these match perfectly with my baby calf-skin stilettos and the "trippy" shade of puke dribbling from my mouth. If it hangs on a hemp rope, save it.

3. **The Last-Minute Porcelain Figurine from China**

And you expect me to believe that when you came across that angel figurine "last month" it just screamed "Nadia G!"? Next time you swing by the dollar store on your way to my house, stop by the gas station instead and get me some cigarettes.

4. **Re-Gifted Cheap Bubble Bath**

Who doesn't love relaxing in a tub full of expired Polyquaternium 7, Methylparaben, EDTA, DMDM, Hydantoon, F.D.&C. Yellow #5?! How luxurious!

5. **CDs from the Uncle Who Thinks He's Hip**

Somehow my nine tattoos, pierced septum, and nihilistic disposition were a dead giveaway that N Sync's Greatest Hits was missing from my music collection.

6. **The Useless $20 Gift Certificate**

Ah, the gift that forces me to head all the way down to a stinkin' store I never shop at, to browse products I'd never buy, and then be forced to shell out my own cash because $20 won't buy you shit. Wonderful.

MORE
XMAS CAC

I have great memories of Christmas Eve . . . orange peels burning in the fireplace, the family singing Sinatra, my father holding back my uncle as he lunged to strangle my cousin . . . man, those were the days!

But things have changed. Christmas isn't what it used to be. Even the kids are different. The other day, I was babysitting my six-year-old cousin. Being that it's the holiday season and all (and I had run out of Ritalin), I asked her to write a letter to Santa. She wrote:

Dear Santa,
Please bring me everything I want for X-mas:
A cell phone, a training bra and makeup!
XO Veronica
P.S.: I love you very much.

It made me so sad. What's the world coming to? Everybody knows that first you have to say "I love you" then you say "Give me what I want." Not the other way around!

DEFLATE YOUR MATE

ong-term relationships are a beautiful thing—as the years go by, your comfort level flourishes, your sense of security grows . . . but most of the time, so does your partner's ass. That's why this chapter is devoted to deflating-your-mate, because you care, and let's face it, walrus lovin' ain't pretty.

When your partner starts packing the pounds, it's rough. You're stuck between a rock and a squishy place. But before you harpoon 'em and dump 'em off at SeaWorld, tap into your sensitive side and think about why they're fondling the deep-fried cheese. Are they depressed? Stressed? Do they hate you? Whatever the case may be, healthy eating helps, and these low-fat recipes are the first waddle on the road to recovery.

The trick to cooking light is to use punchy flavors that'll make up for the lack of greasy goodness. Compensation is key. But you know this already; I mean your mate may jiggle spontaneously but they compensate by being the only one you can boss around. The same logic applies to these meals: There may be very little fat, but the hearty vegetables and aromatics make them work.

Help support your *musholite lover by sneaking these recipes into your culinary repertoire. At the end of the day, it's worth the effort—it's easier to fix a scratch than it is to get a new car. Think about it: If you dump Sasquatch for a sleeker model, you'll have to lure them in with massages, pretend to listen, wear thongs . . . it's a long process to train a new mate, and quite frankly, why bother when you've already got one that vacuums?

LOVE IS ONLY BLIND FOR BLIND PEOPLE

MEDITERRANEAN
CHICK PEA STEW

Some of you may be part of that "no carbs" cult when it comes to dieting, but let's face it, a life without carbs is a life not worth living. When pounds need to be shed it's all about eating smaller portions, getting lots of exercise and going on three-day amphetamine benders. Onto the stew.

Servings: 3–4

ROASTED GARLIC

- Preheat the oven to 400°F. Grab a whole garlic bulb, remove the papery skin from the outside, but keep the skin of the cloves intact. Chop ¼-inch off the top of the bulb. Drizzle with 1 teaspoon of olive oil. Wrap tightly in foil and bake for 35 minutes.

CHICKPEA STEW

- Heat a large saucepan on medium heat, then add 1 tablespoon olive oil, scallions, red bell pepper, and a small pinch each of cumin, paprika, and hot chile flakes. Sauté for 8 minutes.
- Hand crush the San Marzano tomatoes and add them to the pan. Throw in 4 cloves of the roasted garlic (roasted garlic is much milder than fresh garlic), and big pinches of lemon zest and brown sugar. Add a small pinch of sea salt and freshly cracked pepper to taste.
- Let simmer for 15 minutes. In the last 5 minutes, rinse chickpeas and drop them in. Heat through.

SHKIAFFING IT TOGETHER

- Ladle the stew into big bowls. Garnish with a big pinch of finely chopped fresh mint, a handful of fresh minced parsley and a small pinch of lemon zest. Serve with toasted whole wheat pita wedges.

Grocery List

- Garlic (1 bulb)
- Extra virgin olive oil (1 teaspoon plus 1 tablespoon)
- Scallions (3, finely sliced)
- Red bell pepper (1, julienned)
- Cumin
- Paprika
- Hot chile flakes
- Whole San Marzano tomatoes (795ml can)
- Fresh lemon (1, for zesting)
- Brown sugar
- S&P
- Chickpeas (425g can)
- Fresh mint (finely chopped)
- Fresh parsley (minced)
- Whole wheat pita bread (2 pieces)

Gear

- Aluminum foil
- Saucepan

Cumin is a pungent, nutty spice with a very earthy flavor. It is used often in Mexican and Indian dishes, but I like to use it for revenge! I once sprinkled 20 kilos of cumin on my enemy. While he was sneezing, coughing, and suffering from indigestion, I stole from him two scooters and fourteen sheep. It is not what you are thinking! Not for the sex . . . for the companionship! Facebook, Shesh Besh, talking . . .

MANGO CHICKEN SALAD

Having trouble getting your mate off the couch? Don't worry, there're plenty of ways to get poofypants away from the TV! Try running around covered in mayonnaise until they chase you for a lick! Or, you could throw baby cacti at them until they're forced to attack you. Your imagination is the only limit!

Servings: 2

CHICKEN MARINADE

- In a food processor, combine yogurt, garlic, peeled ginger, 1 cup cilantro, and a small pinch of sea salt and freshly cracked pepper to taste. Blend until smooth.
- Pour the marinade into a large ziplock bag. Rinse the chicken breasts and pat dry. Add breasts to the marinade, smush them around, and place the bag in the fridge for 24 hours.

LIME-CILANTRO DRESSING

- In a jar combine the juice of 2 limes, olive oil, honey, and Dijon mustard. Add a big pinch of finely chopped fresh cilantro, a small pinch of garlic, 1 teaspoon minced jalapeno pepper flesh (add seeds if you like it hot), a small pinch of sea salt, and lots of freshly cracked pepper. Cover the jar and shake until thick.

SHKIAFFING IT TOGETHER

- Heat the grill to high and sear marinated chicken for 2 minutes per side. Turn grill to medium-low and cook for an additional 5 to 6 minutes per side.
- In a bowl combine slices of ripe yellow mango and ripe avocado. Drizzle with 2 tablespoons of dressing and mix to coat.
- Add chicken breast to the fruit, and serve with a side of brown rice (optional).

Grocery List

- Low-fat plain yogurt (2 cups)
- Garlic (3 cloves plus a little extra, degermed)
- Fresh ginger (1 tablespoon, peeled)
- Fresh cilantro (1 cup plus a little extra, chopped)
- S&P
- Chicken breasts (2)
- Limes (2)
- Extra virgin olive oil (2 tablespoons)
- Honey (1 tablespoon)
- Dijon mustard (½ teaspoon)
- Jalapeno pepper (1)
- Ripe mangos (3)
- Ripe avocado (1)
- Brown rice, optional

Gear

- Food processor
- Jar
- Grill (if you don't have a grill you can use a large frying pan)
- Mixing bowl

WAYS OF THE SEQUINED TIGER

It isn't easy to confront your lover about their weight. That's why you must harness the power of the Sequined Tiger . . .

You need strong mind...

PEPPER-CRUSTED TERIYAKI TUNA
& WASABI SMASHED POTATOES

This tuna dish is fucking *gourmet* (not to mention, low-fat). The only downside is that the searing process creates *a lot* of smoke, so blast the stove vent and open a window when you're making it. Or better yet, get your Rotund Romeo to frantically fan the frying pan while you're cooking—that'll help burn some extra calories for sure.

Servings: 2

TERIYAKI SAUCE

- Heat a saucepan on medium. Combine white wine, toasted sesame oil, soy sauce, honey, garlic cloves, and peeled ginger. Stir the mixture well.
- Bring to a boil, then reduce heat to low. Simmer for 5 minutes, then take off the heat. Remove garlic and ginger, pour sauce into a small bowl and set aside.

WASABI SMASHED POTATOES

- Wash and peel the potatoes. Chop in equal-sized chunks and boil in salted water until fork tender (about 15 minutes). Drain.
- Roughly smash potatoes with soy milk, wasabi paste, a small pinch of sea salt, and freshly cracked pepper to taste. Don't overmix otherwise they'll be pasty, and pasty mashed potatoes suck.
- Place your portion in another bowl and add ½ teaspoon of unsalted butter. Don't tell.

TUNA STEAKS

- Massage both sides of the tuna steaks with lots of fresh, coarsely ground black pepper. Brush with some of the teriyaki sauce. (Don't use too much sauce, you'll be needing it later to drizzle on the tuna steaks when serving.)
- Heat a sauté pan on high and add canola oil. Make sure the pan is extremely hot and beginning to smoke before adding the tuna.
- Add tuna steaks and sear for 2 minutes on one side—don't move it. While it sears, brush the exposed side with the teriyaki sauce, then flip it over and cook 1 more minute. (This is for a medium-rare tuna steak.)

SHKIAFFING IT TOGETHER

Slice tuna steaks in strips, place them on plates. Drizzle with 1 tablespoon teriyaki sauce, and add 1 scoop wasabi mashed potatoes on the side. Top with a handful of finely sliced scallion greens.

Grocery List
- Dry white wine (¼ cup)
- Toasted sesame oil (1 teaspoon)
- Low-sodium tamari soy sauce (2 tablespoons)
- Honey (2 tablespoons)
- Garlic (2 cloves, peeled, halved, and degermed)
- Fresh ginger, peeled (2 1-inch knobs)
- Russet potatoes (3)
- Soy milk (1 tablespoon)
- Wasabi paste (½ teaspoon)
- S&P
- Sushi-grade tuna steaks, cut 1 inch thick (2)
- Canola oil (1 tablespoon)
- Scallions (handful, finely chopped)

Gear
- Small saucepan
- Small bowl
- Sauté pan

Bro, in Greece we have a saying: "Tuna may be da king of all fish, but not all kings have pointy shoes." When you wanna eat a rare tuna steak it's gotta be sushi grade, and you'll only find sushi-grade tuna at good fish markets. But be careful bro, you gotta make sure dat tuna is fresh too, because if it's not fresh your wife is gonna get mad at you. She's gonna scream at you: "You're good for nutting! You can't even bring home fresh tuna! Why did I marry you?! WE SHOULD'VE STAYED COUSINS!!!"

. . . Just make sure it's fresh, bro. No pearly discolorations, no strong fishy smell, no fights.

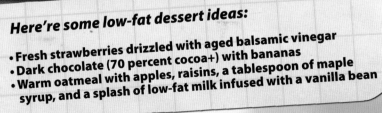

Here're some low-fat dessert ideas:

- Fresh strawberries drizzled with aged balsamic vinegar
- Dark chocolate (70 percent cocoa+) with bananas
- Warm oatmeal with apples, raisins, a tablespoon of maple syrup, and a splash of low-fat milk infused with a vanilla bean

WORKING OUT WITH HANS

I invented this patented workout system years ago. It targets four major muscle groups through five sets of fifteen repetitions. I call it: **"FOUR MUSCLE GROUPS TARGETED BY FIVE SETS OF FIFTEEN REPETITIONS."®™**

5 SETS OF 15 CRUNCHES ®™
Smile baby, you're doing crunches. Flex those muscles.

5 SETS OF 15 PUSHUPS ®™
When doing pushups it's important to keep your body straight and get greased up, so you're more aerodynamic.

5 SETS OF 15 LUNGES ®™
Always do lunges slowly, in front of a mirror, with a really intense look on your face.

5 SETS OF 15 SQUATS ®™
Spread your legs and bend your knees until your thighs are parallel to the floor. Up and down, up and down, 15 times, for 5 sets.

CHAPTER. 14

Valentine's Day

The origins of St. Valentine's Day are obscure. So obscure that in 1969 it was axed from the church calendar because the dated tale "lacked credibility" and was deemed to be of "purely legendary origin." Pick your battles, I guess. The one thing we do know, however, is that it's all about celebrating the one you love . . . to torture. Real love isn't about the joy you get from giving your lover flowers! It's about the joy you get from giving them wedgies! Strong bonds aren't made gazing into each others' eyes, *hell no!* Strong bonds are made with electrical tape and submission holds as you grapple for the remote!

Ahh, love—the endless bickering, the Dutch ovens, the calculated assault of freezing hands on a warm, sleeping body. You have to cherish the one you want to bug until the end of time, and that's what this chapter is all about.

On the flip side, there is a lot to complain about when it comes to Valentine's Day: It's too commercial, it's too depressing, turnips are evil . . . I know. But you know what the worst thing is about Valentine's Day? It's become a Communist holiday! That's right, a *Communist holiday!* Did you know that these days if kids want to give out valentines, they have to give one out to *everyone* in their class? What kind of values are we teaching our children? Back when I was a kid, you had to fight *hard* to get to the top of a stack of valentines! You had to be smart, funny . . . throw a good spin-the-bottle party! Today, "Everybody's special!" Why don't we just axe competitive capitalism altogether and pay hippies and brain surgeons the same wages: two loaves of bread and a gold freakin' star? You know *why* we don't do that? Because you need to be compensated for your efforts, that's why! No one would sweat twenty-two-hour shifts at the hospital if "Rainbow" over there can write 9/11-conspiracy poetry and get paid the exact same salary. HA!

Anyway . . . onto the love cac.

You may be intimidated by pairing shrimp with strawberries, but trust the Nadster, it's fantastic. If you still don't believe me, here're a few testimonials:

Mary: "Holy shit! This really works. Love it."

Hala: "I'd never think of mixing these ingredients together, but wow! Pass me more sauce."

Peter: "My socks are itchy."

Servings: 2

SWEET SAUCE

- In a small bowl, add condensed milk and Japanese mayo. Mix well and refrigerate.

SHRIMP

- Wash, peel, and devein the shrimp. (See Panos's tips on deveining shrimp on page 41.)
- In a small bowl beat eggs. Pour panko crumbs on a plate. Dip the shrimp first in the beaten eggs and then in the Panko crumbs to coat.
- Heat ½ inch canola oil in a frying pan on medium-high heat. Throw a pinch of panko tester crumbs into the oil, when they start sizzling wildly, add the shrimp. Fry the shrimp for approximately 2 minutes on each side. Actual frying time depends on the size of the shrimp, but when you see the shrimp start curving in on itself, it's almost done, so that's when you want to flip it over and fry the other side for 1 to 2 more minutes. Place on paper towels to absorb excess oil.

SHKIAFFING IT TOGETHER

- Rinse strawberries and pat dry. Place 1 shrimp in the center of a plate, add a handful of strawberries and then drizzle some sweet sauce on the side. Tell your lover to combine all elements in each forkful . . . or else.

Grocery List
- Condensed milk (¼ cup)
- Japanese mayonnaise (¼ cup)
- Jumbo tiger shrimp (2)
- Eggs (2)
- Panko crumbs
- Canola oil
- Fresh strawberries (1 cup)

Gear
- 2 small mixing bowls
- Large frying pan

Filet Mignon
with chocolate balsamic reduction

Try cutting your filet mignons into heart shapes before grilling—It'll prove your love (and that you're a nerd.)

Servings: 2

FILET MIGNON

- Bring steaks to room temperature. Massage both sides of each steak with fleur de sel and lots of freshly cracked pepper.
- Heat grill to high, brush steaks with olive oil and sear for 2½ minutes each side, don't move them. Then turn the heat down to low and cook steaks another 2 minutes per side for medium-rare.
- Remove steaks from heat and let rest, covered in foil, 10 minutes.

CHOCOLATE-BALSAMIC REDUCTION

- Heat a small saucepan over medium-low heat and add balsamic and maple syrup. Simmer for 5 to 8 minutes.
- Add 1 teaspoon of finely grated, semisweet dark chocolate. Stir until the chocolate melts, about 3 minutes, and remove from heat. The consistency should be syrupy and the chocolate should coat the back of a spoon. Serve immediately—this stuff gets gummy.

SHKIAFFING IT TOGETHER

- Slap the grilled filet mignon on a plate, drizzle with Chocolate-Balsamic Reduction, and serve with love . . . or french fries. Whatever.

Grocery List
- *Angus filet mignon steaks, 1-inch thick (2)*
- *Fleur de sel*
- *Freshly cracked pepper*
- *Extra virgin olive oil*
- *Aged balsamic, minimum 7 years old (6 tablespoons)*
- *Real maple syrup (6 tablespoons)*
- *Semisweet dark chocolate (1 teaspoon, finely grated)*

Gear
- *Grill*
- *Silicone basting brush*
- *Aluminum foil*
- *Small saucepan*

nadvice

Filet mignon is a great treat for Valentine's Day, but don't ever get fooled into thinking that making dinner is enough. You have to get your sweetie a present, and it's got to be good! None of this cheap-ass "I'll-give-you-a-romantic-massage" bullshit. What do I look like? A raver?! Keep your sweaty paws to yourself!

Wake-up call: Flowers also suck. Who wants to watch a bunch of stinkin' foliage slowly get musholite and die? Not me! Good gifts include boutique chocolates, fancy bathrobes, spa days . . . and cold hard cash.

Don't be afraid. Dark chocolate will add a thick, buttery texture to your balsamic reduction. But it's more than just the texture . . . The bitterness of the cocoa beans, contrasted with sweet-sticky tartness, will layer on the flavor in ways you've only dreamed of.

You're Hot!
(sometimes)

Roses are red.
Violets are blue.
I was desperate in December,
That's why I chose you!

We're Insepurrable

Some people say
we're like day and night.
At times we cuddle,
At times we fight.
But I don't care
what anyone thinks!
Our bond is unbreakable,
We both love to drink.

You Raise My Temp-erature

When I met you
my world was upside-down.
Then I saw your smile
and I was spellbound.
Like a passing rain shower
blessing the ground,
You're the best,
Mr. Rebound!

I Never Want to be A-part

I feel that teenage kind of love,
the kind that's sent from up above.
To not let you know would be a sin!
I'm sorry baby, his name is Jim.

CUT-OUT VALENTINES!

To:

From:

_____

_____

_____

_____

_____

_____

_____

_____

To:

From:

_____

_____

_____

_____

_____

_____

_____

_____

To:

From:

_____

_____

_____

_____

_____

_____

_____

_____

To:

From:

_____

_____

_____

_____

_____

_____

_____

_____

When I am in America, I get caught up in this game called love: the flowers, the chocolates, Santa Claus, and all the other beautiful things that come with Valentimes Day. Some of you may know I have been married thirteen times, but I have only been in love once. . . . Her name was Ashley Jefferson, and she was from America.

She was the squirrel to my nut, the hubcap to my tire, the speaker to my pattifone . . . you get the message. I am telling you this because she left me on Valentimes Day! She said that me paying her cell phone bill was not her idea of "romantic"! But did you know there were over 900 text messages, and two hours of long-distance calls to her mother in Scottsdale, Arizona, on that bill?! Plus, she was charged by the minute, not by the second! They were going to cancel the line if I did not pay the bill! But no! She would rather have a box of chocolates!

Maybe I do not understand America, and maybe I never will, but one thing I do understand is revenge! LOOK AT ME NOW ASHLEY! YOU WILL NEVER TOUCH MY SILKY SKIN AGAIN YOU INGRATE! . . . I'm sorry, Ashley . . . I love you.

Pot au Chocolat

For some reason, I simply can't think of anything clever to write in regards to Pot au Chocolat. Instead, I'll just use this space as a reminder to call your mom and wish her a Happy Valentine's Day. It'll make her happy and she deserves it. Especially if you were a "wild teen" and hitchhiked to Santa Cruz without calling for three weeks . . . I'm just saying.

Servings: 4

- Preheat oven to 300°F.
- In a saucepan bring milk and whipping cream to boil over medium-low heat. The second it starts to boil remove from heat.
- Whisk in finely chopped bittersweet chocolate. Keep whisking until smooth. Set aside.
- In a large mixing bowl combine egg yolks, brown sugar, and a small pinch of fleur de sel. Whisk until smooth.
- *Slowly* add melted chocolate into the yolk mixture. Do this one tablespoon at a time, being careful not to cook the eggs.
- Using a fine wire-mesh sieve, strain the chocolate mixture into a large bowl. Use the whisk to push it through.
- Pour mixture into small jars. Cover each jar with foil and poke holes in the foil with a fork. Place jars in a roasting pan and fill the pan with water halfway up the side of the jars.
- Bake for 35 minutes. Let them cool down for 30 minutes and then chill them in the fridge for a few hours before shkoffing.

SHKIAFFING IT TOGETHER

- Place a jar on a small dish and spoon some fine orange marmalade on the side.

Grocery List

- Whole milk, 3.25% MF (½ cup)
- Whipping cream, 35% MF (1½ cups)
- Bittersweet chocolate (¾ cup, finely chopped)
- Eggs (4)
- Brown sugar (2 tablespoons)
- Fleur de sel
- Fine orange marmalade

Gear

- Heavy saucepan
- Whisk
- Large mixing bowl
- Fine wire-mesh sieve
- 4 little glass jars (or 6 espresso cups)
- Aluminum foil
- Large roasting pan

nadvice

If you're single don't sweat it! Make this meal for a friend! As the old Italian saying goes: "You don't need love to be happy, you just need to be rich and hot!"

CHAPTER.15

GEEK GRILLADE

BECAUSE HOME IS WHERE THE WIFI IS

*A*h, the Internet . . . what would we do without it? Go outside and "socialize"? Buy a CD? Actually watch TV? *Pfft,* that's just crazy talk.

I love the Web. You can find anything you're looking for . . . and a couple of things you never wanted to find, like Goatse CX, or mom's *real* income source.

But as much as the Web is an extensive informational buffet, some people take it too far. They believe that the Web has mystical powers—like "If you don't forward this e-mail to ten twits your dog will die," or "If you build a Web site you're destined to become a millionaire"—business plan or not. But it's all good, because the more time these Asshats spend in front of their computer, the less time they spend reproducing.

For the rest of us, the Web is a world of opportunity: MySpace gives those who can't afford a *real* Web site a haven to overuse crappy graphics; Facebook allows us to stalk pudgy nerds from high school; YouTube allows us to waste endless hours on your boss's clock watching Bitchin' Kitchen . . . But that's not all. The Web is also big business; who needs a real job when you can just send Grandma a screamer and—POOF!—there's your inheritance. Work, play, dramatic chipmunks—the Internet has it all!

But when you start sporting a greenish computer tan, it's time to log off and eat something with vitamins. That's why this chapter is all about getting outside, firing up the grill, and spending time with your friends—in person.

nadvice

As much as you love the Web, your computer can bring you down. Viruses, spyware, adware . . . the Mac people will tell you it's because of your PC, the PC people will tell you it's because of malicious software. But you know what the real problem is? You! If you can't go online without downloading the latest porn smilies and then you complain that your homepage is hijacked, maybe you should stay away from technology, buy a box of fucking crayons, and call it a day.

SPICY BEEF KEBABS WITH MINT

My two favorite things in this world are paprika and Toby Maguire. Paprika because of his texture . . . and Toby Maguire because of his texture . . .

Now that I've grilled the comp-tards, let's move onto some juicy beef skewers . . .

Servings: 4–6

MEAT MIXTURE

- In a large bowl, combine ground beef, minced onions, ½ cup minced mint leaves, cilantro, ginger, green chile, ground cumin, ground coriander, paprika, cayenne, sea salt, and lots of freshly cracked pepper. Mix, cover, and refrigerate for 2 hours.

MINT SAUCE

- Peel the cucumbers, halve them lengthwise, and remove the seeds. Place cucumbers on a large plate and sprinkle with sea salt. Let stand for 15 minutes.
- Drain away liquid and rinse the cucumbers quickly in cold water; pat dry.
- In a small bowl combine scallions, yogurt, ¼ cup minced mint leaves, the juice of 1 lemon, a small pinch of brown sugar, a big pinch of sea salt, and freshly cracked pepper.
- Mix and chill for 20 minutes or more.

SHKIAFFING IT TOGETHER

- Preheat the grill to medium heat. Mold handfuls of the meat mixture around skewers to form sausages. Make sure the meat is an even thickness all around. Brush kebabs liberally with olive oil and arrange kebabs on grill. Cook 10 minutes, turning as needed to brown evenly. Shkoff with yogurt-mint sauce.

nadvice

Kebabs are best enjoyed with an ice-cold pint of German Weissbeer. This brew is sweet with a surprisingly full body, just like your last five e-dates, huh? Add a couple of orange slices for tang, and you're on your way to forgetting about your carpal tunnels.

Grocery List

- **Lean ground beef or lamb (2 pounds)**
- **Onions (2, minced)**
- **Fresh mint leaves (1 cup, minced)**
- **Cilantro (½ cup, minced)**
- **Fresh ginger (1 tablespoon, minced)**
- **Green hot chile (1 tablespoon, minced)**
- **Ground cumin (1 teaspoon)**
- **Ground coriander (1 teaspoon)**
- **Paprika (1 teaspoon)**
- **Cayenne pepper (1 teaspoon)**
- **Sea salt (1 teaspoon plus a little more)**
- **Freshly cracked pepper**
- **English cucumbers (2)**
- **Scallions (½ cup, finely sliced)**
- **Mediterranean plain yogurt (2 cups)**
- **Lemon (1)**
- **Brown sugar**
- **Extra virgin olive oil**

Gear

- **Large bowl**
- **Small mixing bowl**
- **Grill**
- **Skewers**
- **Silicone basting brush**

ZIA MARIANNA'S GRILLED PEPPERS

ℰ nadvice

For those incorrigible uber-nerds who simply refuse to venture outdoors: I recommend an indoor grill. You get almost all the flavor of a BBQ without the nuisance of fresh air or sunlight. The only problem is they create a lot of smoke, so only use if you have good ventilation.

You'll find grilled peppers everywhere, from grocery stores to five-star restos to fast-food chains. But it's lies, all lies! Unless you've had my *Zia's grilled peppers, you haven't experienced real grilled peppers . . . until now.

Servings: 10 (keeps in the fridge for 2 weeks)

GRILLING

- Fire up the grill to high heat.
- Rinse the peppers; pat dry. Throw the whole peppers directly on the grill, charring the skin completely on all sides until they're black on the outside and soft, about 5 to 8 minutes per side.
- Remove peppers from the grill, put them in a bowl, and let them cool down.

SHKIAFFING IT TOGETHER

- One by one, remove and discard the charred skin, the seeds, and the stems. Cut the peppers into really thin slices, ¼-inch thick. Shkiaff them in a Tupperware container. Drizzle with vegetable oil.
- Add garlic, a big pinch of sea salt to taste, and freshly cracked pepper. Mix well and refrigerate overnight.

Grocery List
- Sweet peppers: a mix of red, green, yellow . . . (10)
- Vegetable oil (½ cup)
- Garlic (4–6 cloves, degermed and halved)
- S&P

Gear
- Grill
- Tupperware

ATTENTION CYBERTARDS
a lesson in facebook netiquette

For those of you who aren't quite sure how the Internets work, here're a few rules to follow when on Facebook:

1. Do not randomly post nasty-ass pictures of fat women, fat men, genital warts, fat women shagging fat men with genital warts, or any photo that contains nudity . . . unless it's you; I like a good laugh.

2. I do not give a rat's ass about glittery hugs, inspirational messages, "Have a Great Weekend" template posts, pics of "sexy" men from 1982, or any message that is written in Comic Sans. Save it, or I will punch you.

3. Don't bother sending those "Forward to See What Happens" posts. I'll tell you what happens: I will punch you.

4. Control your burning desire to send chain letters, horoscopes, or chain letters about horoscopes. Trust me. They only bring bad luck in the form of me punching you.

5. I do not want to become a zombie, a pirate, or a vampire; get bought; see who's flirting with me; or hatch a fucking egg, thanks.

Remember kids: The longer the scroll, the dumber the troll.

GRILLED PINEAPPLE WITH RUM BUTTER

nadvice

Enjoy your meal away from the keyboard, but remember: If you don't forward this cookbook to ten of your friends, your boobs may explode!

There's rum, there's butter . . . need I say more? I guess so, because you need a recipe to make it and stuff. Fine. Here goes:

Servings: 1, 6, or 8 (What the hell do I know how much pineapple you can eat?!)

RUM-BUTTER BASTE

- Melt butter in a saucepan over medium-low heat.
- Add dark rum, brown sugar, and the seeds of 1 vanilla bean (slice the bean open lengthwise and scrape out the seeds with your knife). Stir together and simmer 2 minutes.

SHKIAFFING IT TOGETHER

- Slice the pineapple into 1-inch disks. Baste with plenty of rum-butter sauce. Grill on high heat for 2 to 3 minutes per side. You can shkoff this with Crème Anglaise (recipe on page 107) or some vanilla ice cream.

Grocery List
- Unsalted butter (½ cup)
- Dark rum (½ cup)
- Brown sugar (¼ cup)
- Vanilla bean (1)
- Ripe pineapple (1)

Gear
- Medium-sized saucepan
- Grill
- Silicone basting brush

> *All this grilling has got me thinking . . .*

> I have this amazing business idea: Everybody knows that nerds don't work out enough, so I present to you the UNDER THE DESK EXERCISER! Imagine! You could simultaneously work on nerdy things while sweating up a storm at the office!
> To invest, gimme a shout: hans@ bitchinkitchen.tv

CHAPTER.16

BROKE-ASS DISHES

*E*veryone makes some bad financial choices at one time or another. So maybe your Garbage Pail Kids collection wasn't the smartest retirement plan, or maybe Mom was right when she said: "Ma, you idiot! Writing is a hobby!" But as much as being broke sucks, it's an important stage in life. It allows you to appreciate the little things, like the warm smile of a stranger . . . as he stuffs singles into your G-string. It sets you free from consumerism . . . and showering. And look at it this way, you may owe 10 Gs in credit, but you finally have enough points to get that spatula you always dreamed of.

But just because you're broke doesn't mean you can't eat like a queen. With a little bit of effort, you can make something out of nothing (kind of like that "record deal" you've been yapping about for eight years now. Sure, sure, the label will be signing you any day now . . . and *no*, you can't borrow twenty bucks). See, some of the tastiest dishes in the world were created by broke-ass peasants, and Italian cuisine is the perfect example. Pizza, pasta, polenta—all of these come from a time when the ninth kid *was* the side dish.

That's why this chapter is devoted to recipes that taste great, cost little, and give you that extra energy you need to pretend to look for work on Craigslist ;).

✗ nadvice

Remember: Broke people matter. If it weren't for the penniless, we wouldn't have punk rock, reality TV, or anyone to test new meds on! Sometimes you need to hit rock bottom to get to the top . . . and that extra arm growing out of your ass will help you with the climb.

LINGUINE AGLIO-OLIO

nadvice

Aglio-Olio Pasta can feed four
people for under five bucks,
so have a dinner party and get
your friends to bring the booze.
As the old Italian saying goes:
"Give a little, take everything."

Whenever you're feeling as low as your savings account, know that rich people have the same problems you do. It's just that they have the money to solve them.

Servings: 4

PASTA

- Boil linguine in salted water al dente.

SAUCE

- Heat a large pan over medium heat and add olive oil, garlic, a small pinch of hot chile flakes, salt, and freshly cracked black pepper. Sauté garlic for 2 minutes until golden. Take off the heat.

SHKIAFFING IT TOGETHER

- Once the pasta is cooked al dente, strain it, drop it in the garlicky olive oil, turn the heat to medium, and mix it up for a few minutes with a handful of finely minced fresh parsley.
- Sprinkle pasta with lots of affordable Romano cheese (or opt for pricier Parmesan if you're wealthy and just going through that "broke" phase).

Grocery List
- Linguine (450g package)
- Extra virgin olive oil (6 tablespoons)
- Garlic (2 cloves, degermed and minced)
- Hot chile flakes
- S&P
- Fresh flat-leaf parsley (handful, finely minced)
- Romano or Parmigiano Reggiano cheese (½ cup)

Gear
- 1 large pot
- 1 large frying pan

Everybody knows parsley. And if you do not, I wish for peace in your country. But it gets a little bit more complicated than that because there are two kinds of parsley to choose from: The flat-leaf variety, which is best for cooking, and the curly-leaf variety, which is best for drying and selling to tourists.

ZUCCHINI E PATATE

When I was growing up this dish was a weekly winter tradition. Kinda like my dad yelling Italian obscenities at the TV screen during the hockey game because those *disgraziate Canadians scored again.

Servings: 6

- Heat a soup pot over medium heat. Add olive oil, hot chile flakes, the onions (cut in half, then sliced into ½-inch rounds), the green peppers (sliced into ½-inch strips), and a small pinch of salt, and stir. Sauté for 10 minutes.
- Pour tomatoes into a large mixing bowl, crush by hand. Pour the crushed tomatoes into the soup pot, then add a big pinch of sea salt, 2 big pinches of brown sugar, and freshly cracked pepper. Let sauce simmer over medium-low heat 20 minutes.
- Quarter potatoes and slice zucchinis into 1-inch disks.
- In another pot, boil quartered potatoes in salted water until fork-tender (about 15 minutes). Drain.
- To the sauce add cooked potatoes and zucchini disks. Cook about 10 to 15 more minutes, until zucchini seeds start to become visible.

SHKIAFFING IT TOGETHER

- Ladle the stew into big bowls and shkoff with lots of sourdough bread.

Grocery List

- *Extra virgin olive oil (3 tablespoons)*
- *Hot chile flakes (½ teaspoon)*
- *Yellow onions (3)*
- *Sweet green peppers (3)*
- *S&P*
- *Whole San Marzano tomatoes (2 cans, 796ml each)*
- *Brown sugar*
- *Russet potatoes (3)*
- *Zucchinis (4)*
- *Sourdough loaf*

Gear

- *2 medium-sized soup pots*
- *Large mixing bowl*

🖈 CHEAP TREAT

For a cheap and quick dessert, core an apple and place it in a piece of foil. Put 1 tablespoon unsalted butter and 1 tablespoon brown sugar into the emptied core. Wrap the foil around the apple and bake for 30 minutes at 350°F. If you like cinnamon, sprinkle some on, but know that our paths will never cross again.

PASTA E FAGGIOLE

Pasta e Faggiole, also known as *Past' e Fazul* is a staple peasant dish. Every Italian family will have their own way of making it. My mom's side likes this dish more tomato-based, my dad's side likes it more chicken-stock based. To prevent a war, I opted for somewhere in between.

Servings: 4–6

SOUP

- Puree ⅓ cup of cannellini beans, set aside.
- Fry bacon in a large pot over medium heat until crispy. Remove bacon from pot, set aside, reserve grease.
- To the bacon grease add minced garlic and sauté 2 minutes until golden. Add diced onion, celery, and carrots. Sauté 10 more minutes.
- Throw in homemade chicken stock, sweet cherry tomatoes, the pureed cannellini beans, the rest of the whole beans, a big pinch of Greek oregano, the torn basil leaves, and a big pinch of rosemary. Stir well and simmer 20 minutes on medium-low heat.
- Add sea salt and freshly cracked pepper to taste.

PASTA

- In a big pot cook tubettini pasta in salted water until al dente. Drain.

SHKIAFFING IT TOGETHER

- Add a ladleful of tubettini pasta to individual serving bowls, pour on the bean soup, and sprinkle with a big pinch of finely minced fresh parsley and some crumbled bacon. Mix it up and top it off with lots of coarsely grated Pecorino Pepato cheese.

nadvice

No matter how broke you are, NEVER use powdered cheese! Here's a hint: If it doesn't need to be refrigerated, it isn't cheese.

Grocery List

- Cannellini beans (2 cups)
- Canadian bacon (6 strips)
- Garlic (1 clove, degermed and minced)
- Yellow onions (2, diced)
- Celery (2 ribs, diced)
- Carrots (2, diced)
- Homemade chicken stock, see recipe on page 39 (6 cups)
- Cherry tomatoes (10, sliced in half)
- Dried Greek oregano
- Fresh basil (6 leaves, torn)
- Dried rosemary
- S&P
- Tubettini pasta, little pasta tubes (500g package)
- Fresh flat-leaf parsley (1 bunch)
- Pecorino Pepato cheese (or whatever you can afford or steal)

Gear

- Food processor
- 2 large pots

GET FAMOUS FOODS

This chapter is dedicated to the American dream. And nope, it's not Prozac-coated corn dogs. I'm talking about getting rich and famous! Now granted, not everyone wants an unlimited bank account, a penthouse, and a hot pink, vintage mustang with "B1TCH1N" vanity plates, but for those of us who do, this chapter is all about getting there.

People always ask me, "Nadia, how do you get into the entertainment industry?" Well, it's easy! All you need to do is follow these three simple steps:

1 **INVEST A MERE 200 GRAND IN YOUR DREAMS!**
(Bitchin' Kitchen not responsible for emotional damage incurred to get funds. Interest not included.)

2 **DEVELOP THICKER SKIN THAN ZIA'S FEET!**
(Thickening skin may not prevent excessive bleeding due to cutting rejections.)

3 **SPEND FIFTEEN HOURS A DAY FOR SIX TO TEN YEARS PLAYING THE GAME!**
(Following the three-step program may just result in B-list status and an addiction to antidepressants.)

Now that we've exposed how to get famous, let's talk about why we want to get famous. Affirmation, financial security . . . these are all good reasons. But you know what the real reason is? Revenge! Of course it is! To all those people you went to high school with who thought you'd never amount to anything? Tsaketa! Kiss my cookbook, you nerds! To all those producers who dumped your show because you weren't "professional" enough just because you smashed a couple of glasses and got kicked out of the bar! Tsaketa! Drink to that, you stinkpods! To all those in court claiming "emotional distress" . . .

A-hem. So now that we've got our bases covered you'll need some fuel to sustain you through this process. And what better to do the job with than therapy . . . or food.

nadvice

On the long, hard road to getting famous, remember one thing: Never give up! Look at me. I may have sacrificed my family life, relationships, my sanity, but I have a cooking show on the Internet, man! It's so worth it.

California
B1TCH1N

GET FAMOUS FRITTATA

nadvice

Cooking a frittata is like working on getting famous: Slow and steady wins the race. If you crank the heat up too high, you'll burn out before your slimy, yellow insides ever feel the warmth of recognition . . . It's cold in here.

Now I know some of you may be thinking: "Ma, if I'm trying to get famous, why do I need to eat a freakin' frittata?" Well for starters, a solid diet of nicotine and self-loathing needs to be topped off with some protein every once in a while. Second, it's a cheap filler, kind of like your agent's opinion of *you*. And last, these eggs are a glimpse into your starry future: guaranteed laid and cracked.

Servings: 2

POTATOES

- Peel and dice a Yukon Gold potato into ¼-inch cubes. Bring a pot of salted water to a boil. Add the potatoes and cook until fork-tender (about 8 to 10 minutes); strain and set aside.

FRITTATA MIXTURE

- In a mixing bowl combine eggs, a splash of milk, chives, a small pinch of hot chile flakes, a small pinch of sea salt, and freshly cracked pepper. Beat well, then add the cooked potatoes and mix some more.
- Heat olive oil in a nonstick pan over medium heat and add the frittata mixture.
- Turn the heat down to medium-low, cook 10 minutes, flip over the frittata, and cook another 3 to 5 more minutes.

PLATING

- Slice the frittata into wedges and pile it up high—because that's the clichéd key to professional presentation. Then shkoff with jaded resentment . . . or ketchup.

Grocery List
- *Yukon Gold potato (1)*
- *Eggs (6)*
- *Whole Milk, 3.25% MF*
- *Chives (handful, finely chopped)*
- *Hot chile flakes*
- *S&P*
- *Extra virgin olive oil (1 tablespoon)*

Gear
- *Medium-sized pot*
- *Medium-sized mixing bowl*
- *Medium-sized nonstick frying pan*

Let it be known that I hate chives! Why? Because I hate onions. And where I come from, when you have an enemy you curse him and all his family.

But that is another chapter, so let me tell you a story about my friend Avi Ziao who tried to swim to Hollywood with nothing but Speedos and the dream of becoming the next great Hollywood actor—he never made it. He got tired when he reached the New York shoreline and now works at Yossi Towing on Broadway and 4th. Then he met a nice boy, got married, and had two dogs. You see: If you aim for the stars, you may reach the moon! Look at Avi, he may not be famous, but he has his green card!

WATERMELON FETA SALAD

Don't dress for the job you have, dress for the job you want. The same applies to eating. Seeing that stars have eccentric culinary tastes, this Watermelon Feta Salad will have you fitting right in when the director yells for his "Caramelized-bean-sprout-lassie-with-non-fat-camel's-milk-I-SAID-CAMEL'S-MILK-YOU-USELESS-MINION!!!"

Servings: 4

- Remove the rind and slice the watermelon into bite-size wedges.
- Stack 10 mint leaves on top of each other, roll into a cigar shape from tip to stem, and then use a sharp knife to slice them into rounds, creating a "chiffonade" (thin long strips).
- Slice a red onion into superthin, almost transparent slivers and separate into rings.
- Crumble the feta.

SHKIAFFING IT TOGETHER

- Place a cup of watermelon on a plate. Add the rings from one onion slice, sprinkle lots of mint chiffonade, and 1 to 2 tablespoons of crumbled feta. Then drizzle on a tablespoon of olive oil and a big squirt of fresh lemon over the top.

Grocery List
- *Ripe watermelon (1)*
- *Fresh mint (1 bunch)*
- *Red onion (1)*
- *Quality feta cheese (1 cup)*
- *Extra virgin olive oil (¼ cup)*
- *Fresh lemons (2)*

Gear
- *Sharp knife*

> Be careful in this business. People will use you. You'll go to LA, some old lady will promise you a TV show, she'll tell you to come over at midnight, "for a casting" she'll say. But it isn't a casting, man, it isn't a casting.

PAPPARDELLE WITH MUSHROOMS, ASPARAGUS, AND PROSCIUTTO

Der may not be any fish in dis chapter, but der's glory, bro . . . GLORY.

There's nothing better than a plate of hearty pasta after a long day of working toward your dreams (or sitting around all day thinking about working toward your dreams.) I know what you're telling yourself, "Ma, this Italian chick thinks pasta is the cure for everything!" Hehehe . . . *it is.*

Servings: 2 Italian servings, 3 regular

PASTA

- Bring a pot of salted water to a boil. Add half a package of pappardelle and boil until almost al dente, about 8 minutes. (It'll finish cooking in the sauce.) Strain and set aside.

SAUCE

- In a large pan, heat olive oil on medium heat. Add minced garlic and fry until golden, about 2 minutes.
- Add in ¼ of the sliced red Thai chile (this will be pretty hot, use with caution) and the asparagus cut into 1½-inch sections with the hard bottoms removed (1 bunch is about 2 cups sliced). Sauté for 3 minutes.
- Add the mushrooms. Sauté 10 minutes
- Add cherry tomatoes. Sauté 5 minutes.
- Add a big pinch of salt, big pinch of brown sugar, and freshly cracked pepper. Sauté 5 more minutes and then take it off the heat.
- Throw the cooked pasta into the sauce, turn the heat on high. Mix well with tongs until the pasta absorbs some of the tomato sauce (about 5 minutes).

SHKIAFFING IT TOGETHER

- Slap a bunch of pasta on a plate, make sure there's tons of asparagus and mushroom chunks, then add sliced prosciutto or smoked duck prosciutto and lots of coarsely grated Pecorino Romano cheese.

Grocery List

- Pappardelle pasta (250g)
- Extra virgin olive oil (4 tablespoons)
- Garlic (1 clove, degermed and minced)
- Red Thai chile (1, thinly sliced)
- Asparagus (1 bunch)
- Brown or wild mushrooms (1½ cups, thickly sliced)
- Cherry tomatoes (10, chopped into thick rounds)
- S&P
- Brown sugar
- Prosciutto or smoked duck prosciutto
- Pecorino Romano cheese

Gear

- Large pot
- Large frying pan
- Tongs

Nadventure

I once found a piece of coral shaped like a penis. It was awkward.

WARNING: Gratuitous photo of Nadia G on facing page.

CHAPTER . 18

It's not easy to find the perfect mate. Most of the time good looks and a great personality just don't come as a package deal. That's why it's important to focus on the real things: the inside . . . of their wallet.

So you've met Mr. or Mrs. Right(wing), and what they lack in the physical department, they make up for in Google stock. They're smart, dumpy, and totally loaded. That's right, *totally loaded*, and at least you'll have that in common when you consummate this thing. But focus: You want that joint bank account, so what better way to win them over than with a candlelit dinner for two. Home-cooked meals show you care (about your retirement) and this Gold Digger's feast is just perfect for the occasion—it's fancy, wicked, and above all, an aphrodisiac that'll help you put your mouth where your money is.

Wait. I think I just puked a little. . . . Okay. Now let's pay the bills.
DISCLAIMER: Gold-digging is not for the faint of heart and may have minor side effects such as: nausea, bitterness, excessive drinking, and/or drug intake due to a crushing, soul-sucking depression. If you notice any of these symptoms, notify your plastic surgeon immediately. Gold-digging is recommended only for the very lazy, or those who suffer acutely from a lack of any other profitable talent.

nadvice

These recipes may be on the pricey side, but it's a drop in the bucket once you take half. Remember: It's not who you marry that matters . . . it's who you divorce.

Raspberry Point Oysters & Mignonette

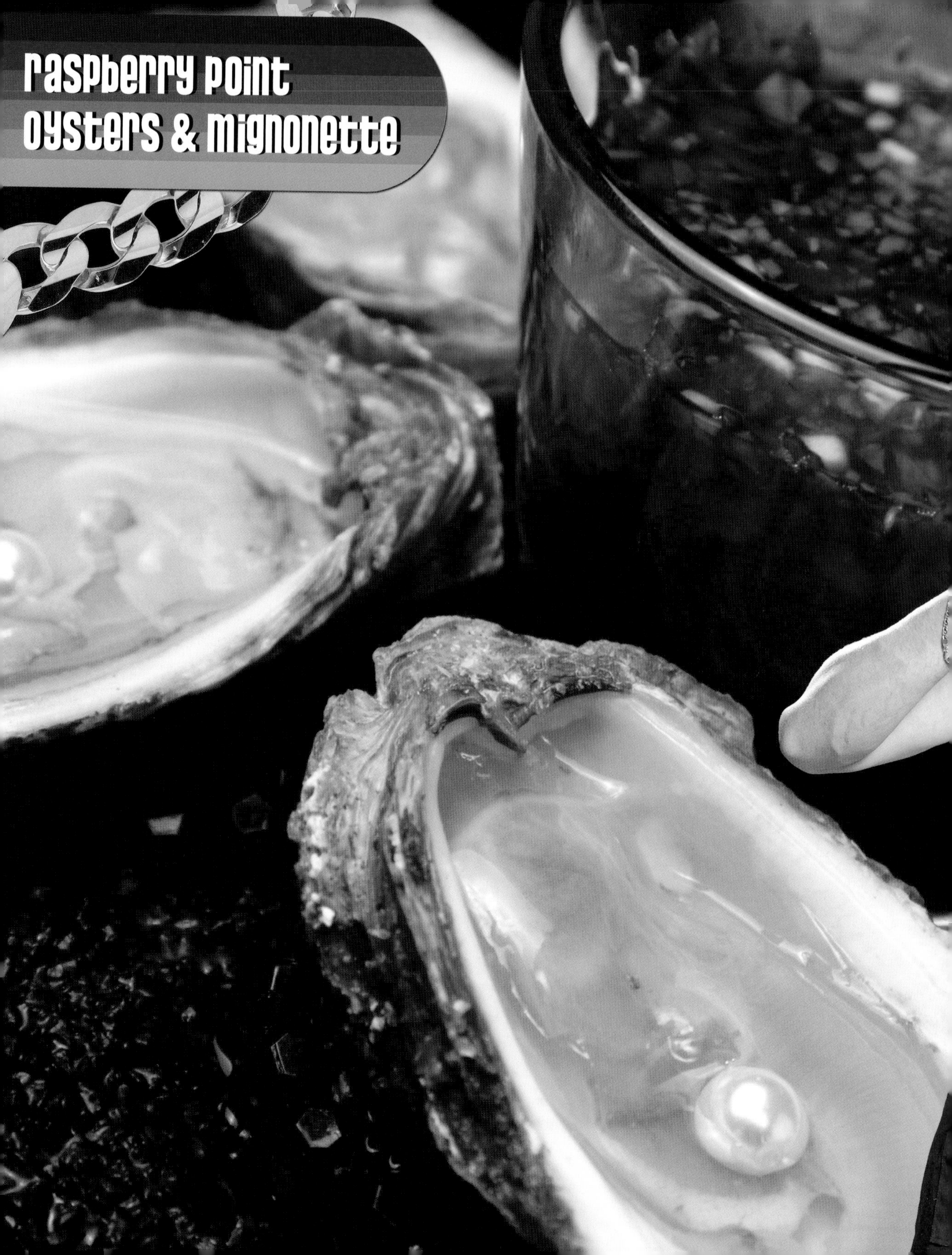

Did you know that each Raspberry Point oyster takes seven years to grow to shucking size? Me neither. I just looked it up on Wikipedia.

Servings: 2

MIGNONETTE

- In a bowl, combine red wine vinegar, shallots, and big pinches of parsley and brown sugar. Add sea salt and freshly ground black pepper to taste.
- Mix well, cover, and refrigerate 1 hour.

SHKIAFFING IT TOGETHER

- Cover the bottom of a large dish with an inch of rock salt. Open oysters and rest them on the salt. Serve with mignonette, a side of freshly grated horseradish, and lemon wedges.

Raspberry Point oysters are a real delicacy, bro. Der silky, salty, and have a sweet aftertaste dat puts da "spb" back in "raspberry." But as good as dey taste, you'll never get to shkoff dem if you can't open dem, so...

Grocery List

- Red wine vinegar, minimum four years old (¼ cup)
- Shallots (1 tablespoon, minced)
- Fresh flat-leaf parsley (finely chopped)
- Brown sugar
- S&P
- Rock salt
- Raspberry Point oysters (12)
- Horseradish (freshly grated)
- Lemons (2)

Gear

- Pretty glass bowl (for the Mignonette)
- Large decorative dish (for 12 oysters)

STEP 1: First ting you need are tools: a shucking knife and an oyster-holder (*minghia, what do I know what dis ting is called?!)

STEP 2: Shkiaff da oyster against da holder wit da hinge of da oyster facing da outside. Den, stick da knife in near da hinge.

STEP 3: Really work dat blade into da hinge of da oyster, bro. Once da blade is in, keep twisting until da hinge pops open.

STEP 4: Glide da blade along da roof of da oyster shell, cutting tru da muscle. Dis frees da top shell and da oyster meat so you can slurp it up. And dat's it.

PORTERHOUSE STEAK
WITH FRENCH-FRIED ONIONS
& ROASTED CHERRY TOMATOES

This recipe is killer: a juicy chunk of prime beef, topped with crispy french-fried onions and a side of glistening roasted tomatoes. All meals should be like this one! I mean it, the faster you clog up those arteries, the faster you get that inheritance.

Servings: 2

ROASTED TOMATOES

- Preheat oven to 425°F.
- In a baking dish combine the sweet cherry tomatoes, garlic, olive oil, and fleur de sel and freshly cracked pepper to taste.
- Mix well, then place tomatoes in a single layer in baking dish and roast for 40 minutes.

PORTERHOUSE STEAK

- Always bring steaks to room temperature before cooking. Pat them dry with paper towels, then massage them with fleur de sel and freshly cracked pepper.
- Sear steaks on high heat for 3 minutes per side. Then lower the heat to medium and grill for another 8 minutes per side (medium-rare).
- Place steaks on a dish, cover with foil, and let them rest for 10 minutes.

FRENCH-FRIED ONIONS

- Cut onion in half. Slice into super-thin ⅛-inch pieces. Separate rings.
- Throw onion into a bowl filled with milk. Let it soak for 5 minutes, then strain.
- Dump flour on a large plate, run the onions through it with a fork. Remove clumps.
- Heat 1-inch canola oil in a frying pan on medium. Fry in small batches for 5 minutes until onion slivers are crisp and golden brown. Drain on paper towels.

SHKIAFFING IT TOGETHER

- Place the grilled steak on one side of the plate, and top with a handful of french-fried onions. Add roasted tomatoes to the other side and drizzle them with a teaspoon of aged balsamic. (You can also mix the roasted tomatoes with a big pinch of brown sugar and balsamic before you plate them to make them sweeter and more ketchup-like.) Serve with a glass of dry red wine and a small bowl of steak spice on the side.

Grocery List
- Cherry tomatoes (20, halved)
- Garlic (2 cloves, halved and degermed)
- Extra virgin olive oil (3 tablespoons)
- Fleur de sel
- Fresh cracked pepper
- Aged Porterhouse steaks, 1¼-inch thick (2)
- White onion, large (1)
- Whole milk, 3.25% MF (1 cup)
- Flour (½ cup)
- Canola oil
- Aged balsamic vinegar
- Steak spice (optional)

Gear
- Shallow baking dish
- Grill
- Aluminum foil
- Mixing bowl
- Large plate
- Saucepan
- Frying pan

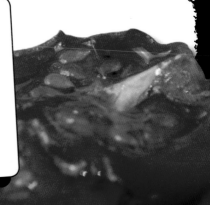

For me a steak is not a steak without steak spice. But what exactly is "steak spice"? Your government does not want you to know! For the longest time it has remained a closely guarded secret, but today I will take my life into my own hands and unveil the truth.

Steak spice is a mix of kosher salt, garlic powder, coriander seeds, dill weed, paprika, chile flakes, and ground black peppercorns!

If you never see me again, tell my mother I love her and I am sorry . . . I was indeed the one who stole all her nylons in '97 (it was a weird phase).

SPICY CHOCOLATE SOUFFLÉ WITH FLEUR DE SEL

My grandmother used to say: "Nadia, marriage is a miserable state, so you may as well be miserable and *rich*."

Servings: 3

CHOCOLATE

- Melt chopped, dark chocolate in a double boiler over medium-low heat. (If you don't have a double boiler: Add 1 inch of water to the bottom of a saucepan. Bring to a simmer on medium-low heat. Place a thick plastic bowl over the top, and dump the chocolate in the bowl.)
- Once all the chocolate has melted, set aside and cool for 10 minutes.

EGG YOLK MIXTURE

- In a small bowl add 3 egg yolks at room temperature (reserve the whites), brown sugar, and a big pinch of cayenne pepper. Whisk thoroughly.

MERINGUE

- Pour 6 egg whites into a big mixing bowl. Add a small pinch of cream of tartar (if you don't have cream of tartar, you can use a few drops of white vinegar). Whip with a mixer until stiff peaks form.
- You've now made meringue, set aside.

PUTTING IT TOGETHER

- Preheat the oven to 375°F.
- Transfer the yolk mixture to a large mixing bowl. Add 1 tablespoon of the melted chocolate and stir. Repeat this process for the rest of the chocolate. (If you dump in all the melted chocolate at once, you'll end up with scrambled eggs.)
- Slowly fold in the meringue, being careful not to overmix. Fold about ten times (the texture of the mixture should look a little scary and spotted with meringue bits, this is what makes the soufflé light).
- Butter three ramekins, dust with sugar, and tap off the excess. Pour the chocolate mix into the ramekins, leaving a ¼-inch at the top of each ramekin.
- Bake for 16 minutes, *not a minute more.*

SHKIAFFING IT TOGETHER

- Sprinkle the soufflés with fleur de sel and serve immediately. Soufflés fall fast.

Grocery List
- Quality dark chocolate, 65% cacao (1 cup)
- Eggs (6)
- Brown sugar (3 tablespoons)
- Cayenne pepper
- Cream of tartar
- Unsalted butter
- Granulated sugar
- Fleur de sel

Gear
- Double boiler or saucepan
- Set of mixing bowls
- Whisk
- Mixer
- Ramekins (3)

nadvice

here's no shame in being a Gold Digger. Darwinistically speaking, it's imperative that smart, rich people mate with lazy, hot people for the sake evolution. Take this soufflé for example: Eggs aren't hot, they're slimy, kinda inky, but rich in vitamins and protein. On the other hand, we have chocolate . . . eet, smooth, decadent, but with barely any nutritional value whatsoever. Put the o together in the oven of time, however, and TSAKETA! Perfection.

REHAB RECIPES

*S*ome people drink because they're bored. Some drink because they're depressed. Me? I drink because I hate people. Whatever the reason, we all get a little too festive sometimes—happy hours last all night, birthday parties make you wish you were never born, you enjoy a white Christmas and you live in LA. I feel you. One drink turns into ten, and before you know it, you're waking up with a hog-tied stranger and even your mascara is running away from you. Let the hangover begin.

My personal research has shown that the brutality of a hangover has little to do with how much you drank and everything to do with how old you are. So don't blame yourself, blame nature!

HANGOVER STUDY

AGE 21 to 25
In your early twenties a hangover's got nothing on you. A minor headache, a few scratches, a walk of shame. No biggie; pop a painkiller and off you go for round two.

AGE 26 to 35
Things start to get ugly. Besides being physically mashed, the paranoia, anxiety, and regret begin to seep from every stinking pore: "Why did I say that? What do you mean I threw the barstool? Oh man! At the network executive?!! Everyone hates me, I'm a loser . . ." You hide for days, maybe weeks, until the screeching voices of self-loathing get faint enough to do it all over again. But the hangover is beginning to scare you; you start weighing the pros and cons.

AGE 36+
I don't know what happens if you party at this age, maybe you explode. All I know is, you don't see too many forty-year-olds partying, and I'm sure it's not because they don't yearn for a crazy night out. I suspect the severity of a hangover at this age beats you into a bloody pulp of submission. Be afraid, be very afraid.

This chapter is devoted to recipes that'll soak up that liquor and have you feeling somewhat human again. Maybe they'll even inspire you to change your debaucherous ways. Then again, as I like to tell beggars: "Change comes from within." But at least you tried, *and ate some fried food!* Let's get cooking.

SWEET POTATO POUTINE

There's nothing better than fries, gravy, and cheese when you're hungover. The potatoes give you a carb kick (to replace the endorphins you lost along with your cell phone); the gravy gives you protein energy; and the cheese, well man, that's just plain fatty goodness.

Servings: 2

GRAVY

- Heat a saucepan over medium heat. Add 1 tablespoon unsalted butter and shallots, finely chopped. Sauté 8 minutes.
- Add wine, a pinch of dried thyme, a small pinch of brown sugar, and freshly cracked pepper. Stir and simmer (reduce) wine for 2 minutes.
- Add 2 cups beef stock, heat 10 minutes.
- In a small mixing bowl combine the rest of the beef stock and flour. Whisk until smooth. Then pass mixture through a fine wire-mesh sieve to remove any clumps.
- Whisk beef stock/ flour mixture into saucepan and simmer for 20 minutes. Stir often.
- Remove from heat and add ½ tablespoon unsalted butter, a handful of minced parsley, and a small pinch of sea salt to taste. Stir until well mixed. Cover and set aside.

FRIES

- Peel, rinse, and cut potatoes into ¼-inch thick french fries.
- Heat 1 inch of canola oil in a large frying pan on medium-high heat.
- Lightly toss potatoes in flour. Make sure there are no clumps.
- Deep-fry potatoes in batches until crisp and golden brown, about 15 to 20 minutes. Place on paper towels to soak up oil.

SHKIAFFING IT TOGETHER

- Slap a bunch of fries on a plate, add lots of cheese curds, and pour on some hot gravy.
- Eat while zoning out to *Family Guy* reruns.

Grocery List
- Unsalted butter (1½ tablespoons)
- Shallots (2 large)
- Dry red wine (¼ cup)
- Dried thyme
- Brown sugar
- S&P
- Organic beef stock (2 ¼ cups)
- All-purpose flour (1 tablespoon)
- Fresh flat-leaf parsley (handful, minced)
- Large sweet potatoes (3)
- Canola oil
- Cheese curds (1 cup)

Gear
- Large mixing bowl
- Saucepan
- Small mixing bowl
- Wire-mesh sieve
- Large frying pan
- Slotted spoon

nadvice

If you are brutally hungover, get someone to make this recipe for you. (Like the twit with the harelip in your bed—the one you thought looked like Joaquin Phoenix—yeah him, at least he'll be of some use.)

CRISPY MEDALLIONE WITH FRESH ITALIAN SALSA

This pasta will settle your belly and the fresh salsa is packed with vitamin C! Plus the recipe for this salsa is already on page 73, so I can sit back and have a beer.

Servings: 4

MEDALLIONE

- Bring a big pot of salted water to a boil.
- Add medallione (or ravioli) and boil until they start to float; strain and set aside.
- Dip medallione in buttermilk and then coat in breadcrumbs.
- Heat ½-inch olive oil in a large frying pan on medium heat. Fry medallione in olive oil until they're crisp and golden brown on both sides, about 2 minutes per side. Place on paper towels to absorb excess oil, then shkoff with fresh Italian salsa.

Grocery List

- Ricotta-mushroom medallione, or any large ravioli you like (10 pieces)
- Buttermilk
- Italian-seasoned bread crumbs
- Extra virgin olive oil
- Fresh Italian salsa, see recipe on page 73

Gear

- Large pot
- Large frying pan

nadvice

Don't buy medallione or ravioli from chain grocery stores. Always get your stuffed specialty pasta at a bona fide Italian pasta shop. Pasta is best when made by angry old ladies, not machines.

175

BRAIN-DEAD BORSCHT

If you're at the point where you can't ingest solids, the next two recipes are for you. They'll pump vitamins back into your system without needing to chew, and they probably taste as good coming up as they do going down. My thoughts are with you.

Servings: 4

BEETS

- Peel beets and chop them into equally sized pieces. Boil in 3 cups salted water for 30 minutes. Strain beets and reserve cooking liquid.

BORSCHT

- Heat olive oil in a large pot on medium. Add minced garlic and sauté until golden, about 2 minutes.
- Add minced onion. Sauté until onions are soft, about 8 minutes.
- Add 2 cups of the beet cooking liquid, along with chicken stock, brown sugar, cider vinegar, halved celery rib and carrot, and sea salt and freshly cracked pepper to taste.
- Turn the heat down to medium-low. Simmer, covered, for 30 minutes to 1 hour.
- Discard carrot and celery. Add a handful of chopped fresh dill.
- Throw in some cooked beets and top with a dollop of sour cream (if you can handle it).

Grocery List

- Fresh beets (6)
- Extra virgin olive oil (2 tablespoons)
- Garlic (1 clove, degermed and minced)
- Large red onion (1, minced)
- Homemade chicken stock, see recipe on page 39 (3 cups)
- Brown sugar (3 big pinches)
- Cider vinegar (2 tablespoons)
- Celery (1 rib, halved)
- Carrot (1, halved)
- S&P
- Fresh dill (handful, chopped)
- Sour cream (optional)

Gear

- Large pot with a lid

Dill tastes like pickles, but make no mistake: Unlike pickles, you cannot use dill to ward off evil spirits. But you can use it to flavor soups, salad dressings, and sauces. The most important thing to keep in mind with dill is that you must add it at the end of cooking, or the flavor will disappear.

Some people believe that dill will cure a hangover. But as my mother used to say: "The best way to cure a hangover is to not get drunk in the first place, because it will never change the fact that your husband is a loser."

CELERY SMOOTHIE

This celery smoothie is surprisingly delicious, trust me. The celery adds a subtle herby undertone that complements the natural sweetness of the fruit. Don't be afraid: Remember, celery is more scared of you than you are of it.

Servings: 4

PREP
- Juice lemons, discard seeds.
- Peel and roughly chop ripe pineapple.
- Separate celery ribs, discard leaves.
- Peel bananas.

SHKIAFFING IT TOGETHER
- Throw all ingredients in a juicer, add honey to taste and ice.

Grocery List
- Lemons (2)
- Fresh pineapple (1, cut into chunks)
- Celery (1 bunch)
- Bananas (3)
- Honey

Gear
- Juicer

When you're hungover, remember to drink lots of water. And for maximum effectiveness, let it dribble down your chest.

UNDERDOG VEGETABLES

*A*ll my life I've been a fan of the underdog. From punk rock to parsnips, underground is where it's at. That's why this chapter is devoted to the reject foods, the vegetables that people think they hate because all they've ever had was the boiled, watered-down version. Kind of like Nickelback or brussels sprouts—Ugh! Just mentioning them grosses me out. That's why we'll move onto the brussels sprouts.

I'm going to teach you how to make these vegetables taste good, and I don't mean in-law polite: "Oh-it's-very-good-Mrs. Sharpino" kinda good, I mean so amazing that you'll want to wolf these down with a vengeance, highlight-them-at your-next-dinner-party, abandon-the-potato kind of good!

See, when you're dealing with *shkeefoso vegetables, there're only two ways to go about it: oven roasted or deep-fried. That's right, you heard me. I'm not going to pussyfoot around the issue and pretend that you can steam a stinkin' cauliflower and have an orgasmic culinary experience. I'm talking about dousing the *stinkpod in tons of olive oil, garlic, beer batter . . . whatever it takes!

So get your frying pan ready and repeat after me: "I love fried vegetables and I'm not afraid to admit it!" LOUDER! You don't need to be ashamed anymore! Gone are the days of hiding in the bushes, waiting for joggers to pass by so you can jump out and scare the shit out of them! It's your time to shine . . . with grease. Let's get cooking.

Underdog Vegetables are just like punk-rock boyfriends. They always perform better when they're a little fried.

PARSNIP CHIPS with sour cream & green onion dip

The parsnip is the shunned albino cousin of the carrot. It has more vitamins than the carrot and more flavor than the carrot, but nobody seems to care. I care! Because I know that underneath its pale, bedraggled exterior lies a sweetness just dying to come out. That's why we're going to pan-fry these babies until they caramelize and become the crisp, sweet side dish they were always meant to be.

Servings: 2

DIP

- In a small bowl, combine sour cream, scallions, dill, the juice of half a lemon, a small pinch of brown sugar, and a small pinch of sea salt and freshly cracked pepper
- Mix well, cover dip, and refrigerate.

PARSNIP CHIPS

- Heat ¼-inch of olive oil in a frying pan over medium heat. Slice parsnips into ⅛-inch disks and arrange in a single layer in the oil. Fry 8 minutes, then flip them over and fry another 5 minutes, until golden and crispy.

SHKIAFFING IT TOGETHER

- Lightly sprinkle parsnip chips with a small pinch of sea salt, plunge a chip into the dip, and get ready to get compulsive.

Grocery List
- Sour cream (1 cup)
- Scallions (4, cut in finely sliced rounds)
- Fresh dill (¼ cup, finely chopped)
- Fresh lemon (1)
- Brown sugar
- S&P
- Extra virgin olive oil
- Parsnips (6)

Gear
- Small mixing bowl
- Large frying pan

What?! What are you looking at? A man can't take a peaceful stroll amongst the parsnips without being objectified? Shame on you.

183

GARLIC-ROASTED BRUSSELS SPROUTS

When it comes to brussels sprouts, there's only one way to eat these suckers: oven roasted with coarse salt and garlic. The outer leaves crisp up and caramelize, the insides stay nice and tender, they're garlicky and salty. . . . Man, you've never had a brussels sprout like this—unless you've had a brussels sprout like this.

Servings: 4

SHKIAFFING IT TOGETHER

- Preheat oven to 425°F.
- Rinse the brussels sprouts, shave the stems, and remove the outer leaves. Then cut the brussels sprouts in halves.
- Drop sliced brussels sprouts into a large, shallow baking dish. Drizzle with olive oil and add a big pinch of kosher salt and freshly cracked pepper. Mix with your hands to coat and arrange in a single layer in the pan.
- Pop brussels sprouts in the oven for 25 minutes.
- Remove from the oven, add minced garlic, and stir.
- Return brussels sprouts to the oven for another 10 to 15 minutes (until fork-tender).

Grocery List
- Brussels sprouts (4 cups)
- Extra virgin olive oil (3 tablespoons)
- Coarse kosher salt
- Freshly cracked pepper
- Garlic (3 cloves, degermed and minced)

Gear
- Large, shallow baking dish

Nadventure

I've always wanted to produce a real infomercial for some carpet-cleaning product. Then, when that inevitable "this-product-is-perfect-for-cleaning-up-those-little-accidents" line comes up, I'd have the editor cut to some kids. I often dream of presenting this infomercial to the Carpet Cleaner CEO and his team. I'd watch the looks on their faces, and then I'd laugh. Man, would I ever laugh.

BEER-BATTERED CAULIFLOWER CRISPIES

nadvice

Remember: It's not underdog vegetables that suck, it's the people who boil them that do!

Minghia! This batter is too fucking amazing. It brings cauliflower to a whole other level. Warning: You won't be able to stop eating these. I fried a whole head for this photo shoot, then hid in a corner and ate it all. I still feel dirty. Don't look at me.

Servings: 4 (or 1, depends on how much of an animal you are)

BATTER

- In a large bowl, combine flour, onion powder, garlic powder, a small pinch of salt, and lots of freshly cracked pepper. Whisk to mix well.

CAULIFLOWER

- Heat ¼-inch of olive oil in a frying pan on medium. Rinse cauliflower, pat dry, and cut into ¼-inch, flat, bite-size pieces.
- Pour bottle of beer into another bowl. Dip cauliflower pieces into beer, then lightly coat them with flour batter, removing any clumps.
- Fry the cauliflower in olive oil until golden (about 3 minutes per side). Then place onto paper towels to absorb excess oil.

Grocery List

- All-purpose flour (1 cup)
- Onion powder (1 tablespoon)
- Garlic powder (1 teaspoon)
- S&P
- Extra virgin olive oil
- Cauliflower (1 head)
- Dark stout beer (1 bottle)

Gear

- 2 large mixing bowls
- Whisk
- Large frying pan

I like it raw. When it comes to cauliflower I'll either eat it straight up, with a dip, or pickled. For a basic pickling brine, experiment with ½ cup of vinegar, ¼ cup of water, ¼ cup of brown sugar, and 1 tablespoon of kosher salt. Use your imagination to spice it up! I love bay leaves, garlic, and handcuffs . . .

for newbies
essential cooking gear

I'm not going to lie to you: At the end of the day you can still make a fantastic meal with one serrated knife and a medium-sized pan. . . . Then again, both a Benz and a Chevette can get you to Point B. Choose your tools wisely, because the ride counts for a lot.

GOOD CHEF KNIVES
You know a knife is high-end if you shell out over a hundred bucks for it and lose chunks of your fingers the first time you use it. Why would you want to spend a small fortune to get maimed? Because once you get the hang of it, it'll provide you with the smoothest prep experience ever, forever.
- Serrated bread knife
- Small paring knife
- Chef's knife
- Knife sharpener

QUALITY POTS & PANS
Pots and pans should be minimum 3-ply stainless or very thick-bottomed so they transfer the heat evenly. When opting for non-stick pans make sure that they're new and not corrosive. If you're still using your mom's hand-me-down nonstick pans, throw them out, they're probably cancerous.
- 3-quart chef's pan
- 4-quart saucepan
- 8-quart stockpot
- 8-inch frying pan
- 12-inch frying pan
- 8-cup casserole/soufflé dish
- Cast-iron grill (or a Cast-iron grill pan)
- Set of 4 heart-shaped ramekins (see page 93)

TOOLS
- Zester
- Cheese grater
- Vegetable peeler
- Food processor
- Juicer
- Jars with lids (large and small)
- Measuring cups
- Large wooden cutting board
- Set of wooden spoons
- Slotted metal spoon
- Spatula
- Ladle
- Set of mixing bowls (very large to very small)
- Fine wire mesh sieve
- Silicone basting brush
- Colander
- Kitchen scissors
- Wine opener
- Chopsticks
- Pepper mill
- Tongs
- Metal skewers

DRAWER STUFF
- Aluminum foil
- Plastic wrap
- Baking sheets
- Parchment paper
- Large and small freezer bags
- A cool apron

introductory grocery list

Stock up on these ingredients and you'll never say "There's nothing to eat!" ever again. Or maybe you'll still say it . . . maybe you're complicated . . . what do I know?!

FRIDGE
- Dijon mustard
- Mayonnaise
- Toasted sesame seed oil
- Japanese tamari soya sauce
- Canadian maple syrup
- Fresh parsley
- Fresh lemons
- Plain yogurt
- Whole milk
- Half & Half, 15% MF
- Crusty whole-grain bread
- 6 eggs
- Some kind of berry that's in season: strawberries, blueberries, dingleberries (or any fruit, really)
- Parmigiano Reggiano (or Pecorino Romano, or 5 year old aged cheddar)
- Baby spinach
- Fresh cherry tomatoes
- Good jam
- Baking soda & a sliced lemon to absorb odor
- Chicken bones, stored in the freezer

CUPBOARD
- Aged red wine vinegar
- Canola oil
- Extra virgin olive oil
- Aged balsamic vinegar (minimum 7 years old)
- Rice vinegar
- All-purpose flour
- Bread crumbs
- Cacao
- Honey
- Spaghetti or linguine
- Penne rigate (or bowties, fusilli)
- Egg noodles
- Brown/wild rice
- Garlic bulbs
- Onions
- Potatoes
- Some kind of nut: peanuts, almonds, pecans . . .
- Some kind of beans: garbanzo, kidney, black, or cannelini
- 2 cans San Marzano tomatoes (795ml)

SPICE ARSENAL
Always store your spices in a dark place and in airtight containers.
- Cumin
- Paprika
- Hot curry powder
- Black peppercorns
- Hot chile flakes
- Sea salt
- Greek Oregano
- Thyme
- Bay leaves
- Cayenne pepper
- Turmeric
- Rosemary
- Vanilla beans
- Fennel seeds
- Coriander seeds
- Onion powder
- Garlic powder
- Dried basil
- Dried parsley
- Brown sugar
- Fleur de sel
- Dry mustard

WINDOWSILL
- Basil plant
- Mint plant
- Decapitated doll (optional)

LIQUOR CABINET
- Dry wine
- Dark rum
- Cognac
- Scotch
- Vodka

bitchin' *glossary

For those of you unfamiliar with Italian-American slang, here's a glossary of terms & Nadia-isms.
WARNING: Use with caution. This slang is extremely contagious and you may infect your friends.

All kinds: Many, a lot.
Illustrative:
Gino: "Were der lots of babes at da party?"
Tino: "Bro, *all kinds.*"

All worried: Used sarcastically to express a lack of concern.
Illustrative:
"Me, I'm *all worried* about Rachael Ray's lawyers."

Baccala: Salted cod, or a moron.
Pronunciation: /back-a-la/
Illustrative:
"Bro, forget about dat guy, he's a *Baccala!*"

Bey yea!: An expression used to denote certainty. A substitute for "Indeed!"
Pronunciation: /bay-ya/
Illustrative:
Gino: "Did you bring da sangwiches?"
Tino: "*Bey ya!* My mudder made dem dis morning."

Big pinch: A three-finger pinch. The equivalent of a ½ teaspoon.

Boh: Used when one doesn't know the answer to a question, meaning "I have no idea."
Pronunciation: /bow/
Illustrative:
Frank: "Where did Mary go?"
Tony: "*Boh.* How should I know?"

Bourdell: Italian dialect for bordello, meaning "chaos."
Pronunciation: /boor-dell/
Illustrative:
Mother: "Tino! Clean your room! It's a *bourdell!*

Bro: Short for brother, used to greet everyone, regardless of gender.
Illustrative:
Gino: *"Bro,* how's it going?"
Mary: "I'm good, *bro.*"

Brutta figura: To make a bad impression, to disgrace. This is an Italian's greatest fear . . . besides removing the plastic covering from a new couch.
Pronunciation: /brute-ah fig-oo-ra/
Illustrative:
Mother: "You better hide your tattoos at the wedding or you're gonna make a *brutta figura!*"

Cac: Crap, low quality, not good.
Pronunciation: /cack/
Illustrative:
"Pfft! You call dat *cac* an espresso?!!"

Capisce: Italian for "Understand."
Pronunciation: /ka-peesh/
Illustrative:
"I don't care about your baby pictures, *capisce?*"

Casalinga: Rustic, home-style Italian cooking. No fancy plating, big portions, grandma-licious.

Common Mispronunciations:
Note that the sound for "th" does not exist in Italian-American slang. It is always replaced with a "d" or omitted altogether.
Illustrative:
Da: The
Dat: That
Dem: Them
Den: Then
Dey: They
Deez: These
Der/ Dair: There, They're
Dose: Those
Dis: This
Nutting: Nothing
Ting: Thing
Tink: Think
Togedder: Together
Tree: Three
Troot: Truth
Tru: Through

Disgraziate: A disgrace.
Pronunciation: /deez-grats-yea'd/
Illustrative:
"You call dat al dente?!… *Disgraziate.*"

Dishkombomballated: Messed up, drugged, or hungover.
Pronunciation: /dish-come-bomb-ba-lated/
Illustrative:
"When I woke up after dat party, I was totally *dishkombomballated.*"

Che cazzo?!: WTF?!
Pronunciation: /kay cats-o/
Illustrative:
"*Che kazzo?!* You're an hour late!"

Handful: The equivalent of ¼ cup.

Hans: Bitchin' Kitchen's Scantily Clad Food Correspondent. He may be greased-up and chiseled, but don't let his magical sheen fool you into thinking that he's mere eye candy. Not only is Hans a bona-fide foodie, he's also the respected inventor of a patented workout system that targets five major muscle groups through five sets of fifteen repetitions. He calls it: "Five Major Muscle Groups Targeted Through Five Sets of Fifteen Repetitions ™." Grr.

Kerfuffled: Flustered.
Pronunciation: /ker-fuffled/
Illustrative:
"When my mom first saw Hans, she was *kerfuffled.*"

Ma: A word of many definitions:
1. Short for "Mother."
2. Short for "Mannaggia"—an Italian term meaning "Damn it."
3. The Italian equivalent to "But."
4. A great way to begin any sentence.
5. A sound that expresses annoyance when words fail.
Illustrative:
Gino: "*Ma*, where's da tomatoes?!"(1)
Mother: "*Ma*, you idiot! Der right dair in da fridge!"(2)
Gino: "*Ma* I looked in da fridge!"(3)
Mother: "*Ma*, look again!" (4)
Gino: "*Maaaa.*"(5)

Ma please!: A sarcastic turn of phrase that expresses disbelief. The equivalent of: "No way!" or "Get out of here!"
Illustrative:
Tino: "Bro, yesterday I had a threesome!"
Gino: "*Ma please!* Using both hands doesn't count."

Me I: A self-important, redundant way to begin any sentence that would otherwise begin with I.
Illustrative:
"*Me I* love The Kills!"

Mezze i piede: Someone who is infringing on your space. Literal translation: "In between my feet."
Pronunciation: /meds E pee-ate/
Illustrative:
"Get out of da kitchen when I'm cooking, you're always *mezze i piede!*"

Mi: Abbreviation of "Minghia." To be used at the beginning of a sentence to accentuate your forthcoming statement.
Pronunciation: /me/
Illustrative:
"*Mi!* Never mind The Kills, me I love cannolis!"

Minghia: A Sicilian swear word for male genitalia. Depending on your tone, it can be used as an exclamation of surprise, excitement, happiness, anger, sadness, introspection . . . It is as versatile as "Fuck."
Pronunciation: /mean-g'ya/
Illustrative:
"*Minghia!* I can't believe it's not butter!"

Mudder: Mother.
Illustrative:
Tino: "Bro, you're 35 and still living wit your *mudder*!"
Gino: "So are you!"
Tino: ". . . I know."
Gino: "So what's your point, bro?!"
Tino: "I dunno bro, I tink I was just acting tough. I'm sorry. Hold me."

Musholite: Slang for "Mushy." Can be used to describe a texture or a person's character.
Pronunciation: /moosh-o-leet/
Illustrative:
Daughter: "Ma, deez beans are all *musholite!*"
Mother: "At least der not as *musholite* as your husband!"

Nadia G: Your Chefness.

Nonna: Grandmother.
Pronunciation: /no-na/
Illustrative:
"Every Sunday my *Nonna* would give me anise candy and twenty bucks."

Nonno: Grandfather.
Pronunciation: /no-no/
Illustrative:
"*Nonno* would cut the cantaloupe and mumble a lot."

Panos the Fishguy: Bitchin' Kitchen's Greek fish monger. Panos's family has been in the fish business for generations: His father was a fish-guy, his grandmother was a fish-guy, even his great-grandfather was . . . oh nevermind, he was just an asshole. The point is, when it comes to expertly knowing ocean critters (or how to get that "wet-look" with hair gel) Panos is the master of disaster, *bro.*

Pinch: Somewhere between a ¼ teaspoon and ½ teaspoon, solipsistic pain and warm salvation.

Rimbambite: A derogatory term to describe someone who is confused or mentally weak.
Pronunciation: /ream-bam-beat/
Illustrative:
"When I told the network Bitchin' Kitchen was both a comedy show and a cooking show, they just stared at me, all *rimbambite."*

Ruvinate: Slang for "Rovinato," which means "Ruined."
Pronunciation: /rue-vee-nat/
Illustrative:
Husband: "Yesterday I dropped oil on my jacket and now it's *ruvinate!"*
Wife: "That's because you drank two bottles of homemade wine and YOU were *ruvinate!"*

Salam: Slang for "Salami", used to describe an actual salami sausage, or an idiot.
Pronunciation: /sa-lam/
Illustrative:
"Stop hogging all da *salam,* you *salam!"*

San Marzano tomatoes: A variety of plum tomatoes grown in the volcanic soil of San Marzano (near Napoli), Italy. San Marzanos are considered to be the best sauce tomatoes in the world.

Sciapite: Weak in flavor.
Pronunciation: /sha-peed/
Illustrative:
"You didn't use enough salt, this sauce is *sciapite!"*

Scraggler: An undesirable person, a hanger-on.
Illustrative:
Wife: "Why da hell is Vincenzo always at our house?! He's such a *scraggler!"*
Husband: "For crying out loud! He's our two-year-old son!"

Shkeefoso, Shkeef: "It sucks" or "It stinks." Can be used as a verb or an adjective.
Pronunciation: /sh-key'f/
Illustrative:
Mary: "I can't eat gizzards or tripe, it *shkeefs* me."
Gina: "Me I tink boiled brussel sprouts are da most *shkeefoso."*

Shkiaff: Slang for "Slap."
Pronunciation: /sh-key-ah'f/
Illustrative:
1. "If you don't stop bugging me I'm gonna give you a coupla *shkiaff!"*
2. "Stop fussing over presentation! Just *shkiaff* some pasta on the plate, I'm too hungry!"

Shkiaffing It Together: Slang for "Slapping it together." This is Nadia G's alternative to classic presentation and plating.
Pronunciation: /sh-key-ah'f-ing/

Shkiatt: Slang for "Explode."
Pronunciation: /sh-key-at/
Illustrative:
Tino: "Bro, I ate tree plates of gnocci! I felt like I was gonna *shkiatt!"*

Shkoff: To eat whole-heartedly; to pig out.
Pronunciation: /sh-koff/
Illustrative:
Gino: "Dat's nutting bro, I *shkoffed* four plates."

Small pinch: A two-finger pinch. The equivalent of a ¼ teaspoon.

Spazzing out: Freaking out.
Illustrative:
"Mary, stop *spazzing out* for nutting! I'm telling you, it's just an ingrown hair!"

Spice Agent: Bitchin' Kitchen's dark and mildly mysterious spice specialist. He hails from Raanana, where the world's best spices are grown. To get to Raanana: exit Ben Gurion, pass Kfar Saba, turn right, turn left, you can't miss it.

Stinkpod: Both an insult and a term of endearment . . . at the same time.
Illustrative:
"I love you, *Stinkpod!*"

Teet: Mispronunciation of "Teeth."
Illustrative:
"I'm gonna punch you in da *teet!*"

Tsaketa: Nadia G's take on the obligatory TV chef tagline or catch phrase. A sound effect similar to "Bam" or "Yum-o", but cooler.
Pronunciation: /ts-sack-it-ta/
Illustrative:
"Now that we've got all our ingredients lined up, *Tsaketa!* Let's get cooking."

Worstest: The epitome of bad, worse than the worst.
Pronunciation: /wurst-est/
Illustrative:
Gino: "Mi, Nadia G's outfit in 'Deflate Your Mate' is da *worstest!*"
Tino: "Bro, you shouldn't say deez tings . . .'"
Gino: "I got no choice, she scripted dis conversation!"
Tino: "Good point, bro."

Yammena: Italian slang for "Let's go!"
Pronunciation: /yeah-men-ah/
Illustrative:
Mary: "Gina, hurry up and tease your bangs or we'll be late for da wedding! *Yammena!*"

Ya okay!: Sarcastic expression that means, "Yeah right!"
Illustrative:
Gino: "When Tino told me his sister was adopted, I was like: *Ya okay!* She has the exact same mustache."

Yeheskel: The Spice Agent's given name.
Pronunciation: Unknown.

You're gonna die: Creepy abbreviation for "You're going to die of laughter."
Illustrative:
"You've never seen *Wonder Showzen?*! Bro, you've gotta rent it, *you're gonna die!*"

Zia: Italian for "Aunt."
Pronunciation: /zee-ya/
Illustrative:
Nadia G: "When I was a kid I used to tease my *Zia* about her weight. With great patience she'd say: 'T'impicca come una capra.' . . . Direct translation: 'I'll hang you like a baby goat.' Since this would only egg me on, she'd have to pull out the big guns and threaten to never feed me one of her famous sausages again. Now that had me back-pedaling, *fast*. What can I say? It's an Italian thing."

index

Scratch & Sniff
metric conversion tables!

Ever wonder what the metric system smells like? Find out by scratching and sniffing the measurements below! Seventy-four different measurements, one mysteriously paper-like scent!

LIQUID INGREDIENTS

U.S. MEASURES	METRIC	U.S. MEASURES	METRIC
¼ TSP.	1.23 ML	2 TBSP.	29.57 ML
½ TSP.	2.36 ML	3 TBSP.	44.36 ML
¾ TSP.	3.70 ML	¼ CUP	59.15 ML
1 TSP.	4.93 ML	½ CUP	118.30 ML
1¼ TSP.	6.16 ML	1 CUP	236.59 ML
1½ TSP.	7.39 ML	2 CUPS OR 1 PT.	473.18 ML
1¾ TSP.	8.63 ML	3 CUPS	709.77 ML
2 TSP.	9.86 ML	4 CUPS OR 1 QT.	946.36 ML
1 TBSP.	14.79 ML	4 QTS. OR 1 GAL.	3.79 LT

DRY INGREDIENTS

U.S. MEASURES		METRIC	U.S. MEASURES	METRIC
17⅗ OZ.	1 LIVRE	500 G	2 OZ.	60 (56.6) G
16 OZ.	1 LB.	454 G	1¾ OZ.	50 G
8⅞ OZ.		250 G	1 OZ.	30 (28.3) G
5¼ OZ.		150 G	⅞ OZ.	25 G
4½ OZ.		125 G	¾ OZ.	21 (21.3) G
4 OZ.		115 (113.2) G	½ OZ.	15 (14.2) G
3½ OZ.		100 G	¼ OZ.	7 (7.1) G
3 OZ.		85 (84.9) G	⅛ OZ.	3½ (3.5) G
2⅘ OZ.		80 G	¹⁄₁₆ OZ.	2 (1.8) G

APPROXIMATE U.S. – METRIC EQUIVALENTS

Credits

BITCHIN' KITCHEN.TV
Created by NADIA GIOSIA and JOSHUA DORSEY
Nadia G — NADIA GIOSIA
Panos the Fishguy — PETER KOUSSOULAS
Spice Agent — BEN SHAOULI
Hans — BART ROCHON

BITCHIN' KITCHEN COOKBOOK
Written by NADIA GIOSIA
Spice Agent written with BEN SHAOULI
Design, Style, and Photography Concept by NADIA GIOSIA
Graphic Design by NADIA GIOSIA and SHERYL KOBER
Produced and Directed by JOSHUA DORSEY
Production Assistance by AUDE SCHNEIDER and SAHAR COHEN

photography
MARTIN BOUGIE — Principal photography of Nadia G, Panos, Spice Agent, and Hans
martinbougie.com

MICHAEL LEVY — Principal photography of food, ingredients, dolls, and objects
michaellevyproductions.com

SUSAN MOSS — Photography of Nadia G for "Single Life," "Halloween Hootenanny," and "Sex-Life Savers," elements on the Bitchin' Kitchen set, abstracts and macros
susanmossphotography.com

DAVID CURLEIGH — Photography of Nadia G for "Impress the Inlaws," "Makeup Soups," and "Rehab Recipes"
davidcurleigh.com

makeup, hair and styling
SANDRA TRIMARCO — Principal hair and makeup for Nadia G and secondary characters; Principal Stylist with Nadia G
sandratrimarco.com

ROBERTO BUONO — Hair for "Get Famous"
MARY MARTINELLI — Makeup and SPFX makeup for Nadia G for "Halloween" and "Sex-Life Savers"
ASHLEY BILODEAU — Hair for "Halloween" and "Sex-Life Savers;" stylist with Nadia G for same, as well as contributing stylist for "Geek Grillade"
AUDE SCHNEIDER — Contributing stylist for "Underdog Vegetables," "Valentines," "Broke-Ass," and others
CATHERINE LANIEL — Back tattoos on Nadia G for "Break-Up Bonanza"
makeupzone.ca

food
NADIA GIOSIA — Cooking and food stylist
AUDE SCHNEIDER — Food prep and contributing stylist
THEO DIAMANTIS of OENOPOLE — Sommelier for wine choices and core descriptions

Art Credits

I'd like to give a major shout out to all the exceptionally talented BRUSH, FONT, SHAPE, PATTERN, and TEXTURE DESIGNERS out there. These Photoshop ninjas make the V2, collective art of graphic design possible and I am truly honored to feature their gorgeous work in this book. Without their skill and generosity the Net Gen art of digital scrapbooking and collage wouldn't be possible.

I thank you from the bottom of my heart. You rock.

Grunging on cover and pp. iv, 1, 98, 100–101, and heart pattern on pp. 129–30 © JASON GAYLOR, DESIGNFRUIT.COM

Office supplies (thumbtacks, paperclips, and more) throughout and stamps on p. 130 © NELA DUNATO, INOBSCURO.COM

Sticky tape © SOMBER RESPLENDENCE

Splatter brush on pp. xiii and 175 © BITTBOX.COM

Beyond Wonderland font on pp. xiv, 2, 4, and 8 © CHRIS HANSEN

Stencil™ Bold font on pp. 6-7 by GERRY POWELL

Martini glasses on p. 7 © GEM FONTS 98

Sparklies brush on p. 18, eagle stamp on p. 25, dripping brush on pp. 80–89, PMS badge halftone décor on p. 81, and green circle décor on pp. 182, 184, and 186 © WWW.BRUSHES.OBSIDIANDAWN.COM

Smoke brush on pp. 20-21 © FALLN-BRUSHES.DEVIANTART.COM

Chawsy font on p. 71 (mwahahahaha) and Digitek and Digital Dream Fat fonts on pp. 134–41 © JAKOB FISCHER at WWW.PIZZADUDE.DK, all rights reserved.

Verve Alternate font on pp. 81–88 by DIETER STEFFMAN

Handpainted ornaments on pp. 106, 108, and 109 © ARTISTRY OF POLAND LLC, WWW.ARTISTRYOF POLAND.COM

Blood splatter brush on pp. 123–33 © GARFCORE 2006~2008

Additional spot art throughout provided by ISTOCKPHOTO.COM and SHUTTERSTOCK.

Thanks

I'd like to thank MARTIN BOUGIE fashion photographer extraordinaire for bringing his slick couture style and true expertise to this punk project. SANDRA TRIMARCO—the best makeup artist in the world. Period. MICHAEL LEVY, whose food photography brought my dishes to the next level, a true artist. DAVID CURLEIGH who saved our asses and made mine look great at the same time. SUSAN MOSS whose gritty and candid style captures the soul of Bitchin' Kitchen. BEN SHAOULI, PETER KOUSSOULAS, BART ROCHON, SIMON WEBB, SAHAR COHEN, MARY MARTINELLI, AUDE SCHNEIDER, UGO GITAU, GABRIELLE VERVILLE, ASHLEY BILODEAU, ALAIN JULFAYAN, SYLVIA WILSON, PAWEL POGORZELSKI, SUGAR SAMMY, STEVE PATTERSON, DEREK SEGUIN, MAUDE DELAGRAVE, STEVE HIGGINS, BLAIR MCKAY @ HDOT NETWORKS, JEAN TURGEON, RITA MONACO, ROBERTO BUONO, CATHERINE LANIEL, MARC GAGNON, ALAIN CHARBONNEAU, AIRBORNE MOBILE, CHRISTIAN RACINE @ CINEFILMS & VIDEO PRODUCTIONS, CHRISTIAN BOLDUC, JODI LIEBERMAN @ THRULINE, CHRIS JACQUEMIN and AMANDA KOGAN @ THE ENDEAVOR AGENCY, ROB RADER, and everyone who worked so fucking hard for so little because they believed in this project.

I'd also like to thank our fabulous editor HEATHER CARREIRO for making the discovery, having the chutzpah, seeing the potential, and championing the cause throughout the entire process of making this book. Big thanks to IMEE CURIEL for her fine-toothed comb and insights. A huge thanks to SHERYL KOBER and her team, for taking on the massive challenge with me of giving graphic shape to this unwieldy book. You are warriors! Finally, big thanks to JANE AMARA for the unprecedented decision to allow me to put my signature on the design of this book.

Thanks to JOSH for poking me out the fetal position a few times when I'd never have been able to do it myself. Josh, without you, none of this would have ever been possible. You're my mentor and best friend.

Much love to my family whose patience, unwavering support and strength fed me and taught me everything I know: My MOM LUISA GIOSIA, THE MEMORY OF MY FATHER JOE GIOSIA, ZIA MIMI, ZIA RITA, VALERIE & VICTORIA, ZIA MARIANNA & ZIO PIETRO, TERRI, ANNA, NONNA CARMELA, NONNO SANTINO, ZIA MARITINA. And equally to Josh's family whose loving care packages, warmth and incredible knowledge of exactly what vegetable is in season at 5 pm on October 3rd never ceases to amaze me: cook extraordinaire TANJA HAHN DORSEY, man-after-my-own-gourmand-heart STEVE DORSEY, and the inimitable DOROTHY DORSEY.

Thanks as well to my Mom and Tanja for all the recipe inspirations, consultations, and food talk.

I'd like to thank our rockin' sponsors: ELMIRA STOVEWORKS for our spectacular appliances, KASTELLA, DADDY-O CLOTHING, BROWNE & CO, KRISTEN FERRELL, CAROLYN'S KITCHEN, NEENAH, LYDIA LUKIDIS JEWELRY, 3FEMMES & 1COUSSIN, OENOPOLE WINES, INDUSTRIAL DESIGN SOCIETY OF AMERICA (IDSA), GAD SHANAAN, ALTITUDE DESIGN, BMW GROUP DESIGNWORKSUSA, ECOPOD, SAECO, GUZZINI, DEMEYERE, CUISINE GOURMET, DICKIES, RKS DESIGN, SEX CITE, BOUTIQUE EVA B, & LIGHTAIR.

About the Author

Complete with stereotypical "fun-loving-author" photo and dry, third-person description!

An early pioneer of skit comedy on the Web, Nadia Giosia has been writing, producing, and starring on the www circuit since 2002. She has several comedy sites, songs, and award-winning webisodes under her studded belt.

This Montreal native grew up in an Italian household where the family-run catering business was always the center of activity. Passionate about both comedy and cooking, Nadia decided to make fun of her cake and eat it too, and Bitchin' Kitchen was born.

In late December 2007 Bitchin' Kitchen won "The Wave Award" for "Favorite Mobile Comedy Series" after its first season on air.

Nadia G is also a graphic designer and runs the boutique design studio "Mult1med1a" in Montreal. *Bitchin' Kitchen Cookbook* is her brain-child.

She lives in Montreal with no stinkin' pets, spouses, or spawn.

Bitchin' Kitchen

You can watch new episodes of Bitchin' Kitchen on www.bitchinkitchen.tv. You'll also find recipes, articles, a community of fierce foodies, and the mysterious Angry Squirrel mascot. (Don't ask.)